D0776764

Praise for *You Need a Leader—Now What?*

"The most challenging and most pressing job in business is connecting the right leader to the right opportunity. Jim Citrin is the world's expert at helping companies thrive and accelerate by choosing exceptional leaders that match the unique needs of the organization to the unique skills of the leader."

—Tim Armstrong, chairman and CEO, AOL

"The core theme of *You Need a Leader—Now What?*—the right individual, right situation, and right process—is spot-on. Board members often forget this. The "insider versus outsider" research is groundbreaking, and the process of how to interview a candidate is incredibly useful. Every board and company should have a coaching session with this book as the guide for how to best do this."

—Greg Brenneman, chairman, CCMP Capital Advisors

"There is nothing more important than hiring great people. Jim Citrin and Julie Daum are simply the best at identifying the perfect talent for high-level jobs, and this book reveals exactly how they go about it."

—Stephen P. Burke, CEO, NBC Universal

"This book is a must-read for anyone—a CEO, a board member, or an HR professional—who may ever become part of the process of choosing a new leader for any organization. In clear and concise language that's backed up by a wealth of research, the authors frame the challenge, provide a road map to success, and offer practical advice. Read it. You'll learn a lot. You'll think a lot. And you'll be prepared to choose the right leader when the time comes."

—Ursula Burns, chairman and CEO, Xerox

"We all know that great people are the key to a great organization. But as Jim Citrin and Julie Daum illustrate, there's much more to it than that. The key is matching the right person to the right situation using the right process. This book will show you how."

—Stephen M. Case, founder and CEO, Revolution and AOL

"People decisions are the most important decisions in your company, yet they're often made with the least rigor. This excellent book supplies rigor plus something even more valuable—wisdom."

—Geoff Colvin, senior editor of *Fortune* magazine and author of *Talent Is Overrated: What Really Separates World Class Performers from Everybody Else*

"Finding the best leader for your organization is often a difficult and lengthy process. This important book offers three essential truths that can help guide and direct you through this puzzle. Through tremendous examples and comprehensive analysis, Citrin and Daum give you the pieces to put it all together."

—Stephen R. Covey, author of *The 7 Habits of Highly Effective People* and *The Leader in Me*

"What could be more important to a leader's success than hiring an incredible team? *You Need a Leader—Now What?* offers readers a comprehensive guide to hiring not just talent but exactly the right talent. A practical process, rigorous research, and fascinating, instructive stories make this book a real winner for anyone who's hiring."

—Keith Ferrazzi, author of *Never Eat Alone* and *Who's Got Your Back*

"Jim Citrin and Julie Daum together bring four decades of experience to explore the maze of issues surrounding the search for a new CEO. Their framework, examples of good and bad practices, and advice all provide valuable lessons for a board of directors seeking to fulfill its most important role—putting in place an effective leader."

—Donald J. Gogel, chairman and CEO, Clayton, Dubilier & Rice LLC

"For boards, CEOs, or anyone managing an organization large or small, the most important decisions invariably come down to picking the right people for the right jobs. Jim Citrin and Julie Daum have distilled a career's worth of experience into this lucid exploration of a process that can help any organization identify, select, and motivate the best leaders."

—James P. Gorman, CEO, Morgan Stanley

"The key to running a great business is matching the right person to the right situation. This wonderful book shows how to make that happen. Written by two of the most successful experts in the field, it's filled with illuminating case studies and very clear lessons. Even if you're not headhunting for new executives, this book is both a delight to read and filled with useful insights on how to be an effective leader."

—Walter Isaacson, president and CEO, Aspen Institute, and author of *Einstein: His Life and Universe* and *Benjamin Franklin: An American Life*

"Much has been written about the art of leadership. Citrin and Daum provide a provocative new lens, upending some commonly held assumptions and sharing a clear and empirically proven road map for choosing leaders who will succeed."

—Andrea Jung, chairman and CEO, Avon Products

"Not only is this book invaluable to those seeking a new leader for their organization, but it is also a must-read for anyone going through the process of being interviewed for a key leadership role."

—Steven A. Kandarian, president and CEO, MetLife

"Choosing a CEO is certainly the most important and difficult issue that boards have to deal with. And choosing a management team is similarly the most important and difficult task for a CEO. In *You Need a Leader—Now What?* Citrin and Daum demonstrate a clear-eyed, rigorous approach to leadership selection that works at the board level and across the organization. This is essential reading for everyone in the people business—which is everyone in business!"

—James M. Kilts, founding partner, Centerview Partners,
former chairman and CEO, Gillette, and author of
*Doing What Matters: How to Get Results That Make a
Difference—The Revolutionary Old-School Approach*

"The most difficult and the most important task any executive or board member can be given is selecting new leadership. He alone can make the difference in success or failure, and there is no reference manual for explaining how to do it well. In fact, it is frightening that so little time or thought is given to this most important decision in companies today. Jim and Julie offer wisdom and pattern-matching experience to help those tasked with this daunting challenge to avoid mistakes that are too often made. I highly recommend it as required reading for corporate boards."

—Ray Lane, managing partner, Kleiner Perkins Caufield & Byers,
and nonexecutive chairman, Hewlett-Packard

"This is a wonderful book for anyone who is grappling with the issues of succession. At a minimum, it should be required reading for board members of private or nonprofit organizations. Through compelling examples of successes and failures combined with great analysis and recommendations on how to approach this crucial process, the authors have created a brilliant manual for choosing leaders in simple and complex organizations."

—Michael Lynton, chairman and CEO, Sony Pictures Entertainment

"An essential book that will make you completely rethink your approach to selecting a leader to run your organization. In *You Need a Leader—Now What?* Jim Citrin and Julie Daum pick apart the myths associated with leadership selection and reveal why conventional wisdom in this area is so often flawed. The choice of a leader is one of the most critical decisions an organization can make. If you are looking for a guide to help you avoid the traps in leadership selection and instead find the *right* individual to lead *your* organization, then this is the book for you."

—Youngme Moon, Donald K. David Professor of Business Administration, Harvard Business School, and author of *Different: Escaping the Competitive Herd*

"Now what? Rethink. This book breaks all common assumptions about the search for succession, destroying the myth that picking a new leader is a matter of finding a hero. Read the book to understand that the right person is most likely not who or where you think. Skills are not unimportant, but choosing the right person is a surprising alignment of paths, perceptions, personalities, and potentials."

—Nicholas Negroponte, chairman emeritus, MIT Media Laboratory, founder and chairman, One Laptop Per Child, and author of *Being Digital*

"Citrin and Daum have written a highly engaging and valuable book on management and leadership. Like great coaches who have seen most every scenario, they are able to guide their players with unusual perspicacity and insight. Their case studies are cautionary and hugely instructive. If you read this book carefully, in whatever field you find yourself, you will make far fewer mistakes and may even be heralded as a visionary."

—Richard L. Plepler, co-president, HBO

"Jim Citrin's and Julie Daum's new book on how to choose a productive leader is a first-rate guide for organizations large and small. They cut through the received wisdom about picking a CEO to deliver a flexible but powerful framework for guiding an organization to a successful succession."

—Michael S. Roth, president, Wesleyan University

"An exceptional, illuminating and insightful book; an evidence-based, best-practice guide, for every corporate and nonprofit board executing the selection of an outstanding CEO; invaluable principles for identifying the 'best fit' leader for navigating the waters of today's currents, who can imagine and execute for a future ahead of the curve. One of the top books on CEO selection, a must-read."

—Dr. Indira Samarasekera, president and vice-chancellor,
University of Alberta, Canada

"There's one big difference between companies that change the world and those that don't: having the right people. *You Need a Leader—Now What?* offers a clear road map for how to identify and select the right people for all levels of your organization."

—Sheryl Sandberg, COO, Facebook

"One of the most important yet challenging aspects of leadership is surrounding oneself with the right people. Although the process is more art than science, Jim Citrin and Julie Daum do an outstanding job of lighting the way with research-based principles backed by true stories of success."

—Howard Schultz, chairman, president, and CEO,
Starbucks, and author of *Onward: How Starbucks
Fought for Its Life without Losing Its Soul*

"For recruiting seasoned leaders, James Citrin and Julie Daum offer a powerful playbook. Based on gripping accounts from extensive executive-search experience in business and beyond, *You Need a Leader—Now What?* tells us that the essence is strategic fit, a tight match of what they bring with what we require and the right steps to make it stick."

—Michael Useem, William and Jacalyn Egan Professor
of Management and director of the Center for
Leadership and Change Management at the
Wharton School, University of Pennsylvania,
and author of *Learning from Catastrophes: Strategies
for Reaction and Response* and *The Leadership Moment*

You Need a LEADER— Now What?

ALSO BY JAMES M. CITRIN

You Need a LEADER— Now What?

How to Choose the Best Person
for Your Organization

James M. Citrin
Julie Hembrock Daum

CROWN BUSINESS / NEW YORK

Copyright © 2011 by Esaress Holding, Ltd.

All rights reserved.

Published in the United States by Crown Business, an imprint of the
Crown Publishing Group, a division of Random House, Inc., New York.
www.crownpublishing.com

CROWN BUSINESS is a trademark and CROWN and the Rising Sun
colophon are registered trademarks of Random House, Inc.

Crown Business books are available at special discounts for bulk
purchases for sales promotions or corporate use. Special editions,
including personalized covers, excerpts of existing books, or books with
corporate logos, can be created in large quantities for special needs. For
more information, contact Premium Sales at (212) 572–2232 or e-mail
specialmarkets@randomhouse.com.

Library of Congress Cataloging-in-Publication Data
Citrin, James M.
   You need a leader—now what? : how to choose the best person for your
organization / James M. Citrin, Julie Hembrock Daum.—1st ed.
      p. cm.
1. Executives—Selection and appointment. 2. Executive succession.
I. Daum, Julie Hembrock. II. Title.
   HF5549.5.S38C58 2011
   658.4'0711—dc22   2011011799

ISBN 978-0-307-58779-4
eISBN 978-0-307-58781-7

PRINTED IN THE UNITED STATES OF AMERICA

Book design by Gretchen Achilles
Jacket design by Daniel Rembert

10 9 8 7 6 5 4 3 2 1

First Edition

JMC:

To My Spencer Stuart partners with whom I've had momentous and memorable work and life experiences in capitals around the world—San Francisco, Berlin, Howie-in-the-Hills, Charleston, Paris, Palm Beach, Dublin, Washington, D.C., Rome, Bermuda, Barcelona, Los Angeles, Lisbon, Orlando, New York, Boston, Chicago, Atlanta, London, Vienna, Sao Paolo, Dubai, Toronto, Frankfurt, and Beijing

JHD:

To my three beautiful, talented, and lovely girls, Alexandra, Schuyler, and Bailey

CONTENTS

You Need a LEADER— Now What?

I.
THE BIG PICTURE

1. THE CURIOUS CASE OF BILL PEREZ

You have a key leadership job to fill. Naturally, you want the *very best person*. But what does this really mean?

Have you ever come across situations in which the same person, with similar mandates executed more or less the same way, could be a spectacular success in one situation and an outright failure in another? What does this imply about how to choose the very best people for your top leadership positions?

This is precisely what we will explore in the illuminating story of an American executive named William D. "Bill" Perez, who rose through the ranks to become the chief executive officer of consumer-products giant S. C. Johnson & Son, and then went on to be recruited from the outside to lead Nike Inc., and then Wm. Wrigley Jr. Company.

LET'S START BY rewinding the clock back to 1959 and head to Beaverton, Oregon, where Phil Knight, a twenty-one-year-old middle-distance runner, starred on the University of Oregon track team. His coach, Bill Bowerman, was obsessed with how to make running shoes lighter and more durable to improve his team's performance on the track. Bowerman's obsession was very much on Knight's mind when a couple of years later, as a student at Stanford Business School, he wrote a paper for his small business class about his concept for a new company. Knight's idea: "Can Japanese sports shoes do to German sports shoes what Japanese cameras did to German cameras?" Knight's premise was that a viable business could be built by importing inexpensive but high-quality running shoes from Japan to the United States. In 1963, after a year of round-the-world travel, which included a visit to Japan, he put his money where his mouth was by investing $500 to create Blue Ribbon Sports Inc. to import Tiger brand running shoes. He persuaded Bowerman to match his seed investment and become cofounder.

As a fledgling entrepreneur Knight went with what he knew. He started selling the running shoes at the University of Oregon track out of the back of his green Plymouth Valiant. In the company's first year, it generated a whopping $364 in sales; but by 1969, Blue Ribbon Sports surpassed the $1 million mark on the strength of a new waffle-pattern running shoe tread that would provide better traction. In 1972, Knight renamed the company Nike, after the mythological Greek goddess of victory. The company's now ubiquitous Swoosh logo was designed the prior year to depict one of Nike's wings and represent "the spirit of the winged goddess who inspired the most courageous and chivalrous warriors at the dawn of civilization."

Over the years, Nike rode the wave of—some would say *drove*—the fitness revolution behind high-profile athlete endorsements, a continuous flow of new product introductions, and the company's cultlike devotion to Knight, who with his ever-present sunglasses and wavy reddish-blond hair was the embodiment of cool. He led the company's initial public offering in 1980, drove the organization past the $1 billion revenue mark in 1986, and was profiled in an August 1993 *Sports Illustrated* cover story under the headline "How This Man Turned a Tiny Sneaker Company into the Most Powerful Force in Sports." In 2004, forty-five years after graduating from the University of Oregon (having become its most famous, wealthy, and philanthropic alumnus), and with the company exceeding $12 billion in revenues, Knight, then sixty-six years old, was ready to turn over the reins.

Both Knight and Nike's board of directors became convinced that the way the company developed products, marketed to consumers, and sold to retail was anachronistic compared with the best practices of the most successful consumer-products companies. The two logical, potential internal successors to Knight, copresidents Charlie Denson and Mark Parker, had grown up inside the company and had little, if any, experience with the world-class marketing techniques used by consumer-products companies such as Procter & Gamble and Unilever. Knight, therefore, felt he had to go outside the company and bring in the person who would be his successor as CEO, conducting a highly secretive search for his replacement.

After reviewing seventy-five résumés, personally interviewing fifteen candidates, and hosting a series of meetings with "the final four" candidates from several of the world's most renowned consumer-product companies, Knight made his choice. It was Bill Perez, a highly regarded CEO, who had spent thirty-four years with S. C. Johnson, the private company founded in 1886, maker of Johnson Wax, Windex, Drano, and Pledge, among dozens of household brands. Even though he had had eight years of experience as CEO of a $6.5 billion global consumer-products company, the announcement of Perez came as a surprise to Nike employees, investors, and the sports industry alike. Perez was a well-respected chief executive, to be sure, but an unknown outsider whose experience with Nike was limited to wearing the company's running shoes as a marathoner. Nonetheless, the choice was seen as evidence that Nike wanted to professionalize its management approach and implement the disciplines of consumer packaged-goods marketing, product development, and market research.

Perez had to overcome his concerns about taking over from an iconic founder, who would remain as chairman, wondering if he would truly be in charge. He also realized that he had to integrate himself successfully into a distinct culture that had limited success bringing in outsiders at a senior level. (To be fair, Nike was no less effective bringing in outsiders to key *functional* leadership roles such as chief financial officer than many market-leading companies.) One senior Nike executive told us, "Nike's culture is so distinct, which is both a strength and weakness, that even if one's cultural radar was very keen, it is easy to make fatal missteps."

Perez had done his homework and tried to address this. "This is going to be a brand-new industry for me," he said at the time of his appointment in late 2004. "I'm used to selling Ziploc bags and Drano." In an effort to mitigate the risk both for Perez and for Nike, Knight and Perez had gotten together for multiple one-on-one meetings and two dinners over a yearlong period. They talked about management philosophies, brand building, their respective corporate cultures, Knight's vision for the company, and how they would work together. At the end of the process, Knight flew out to spend a social evening with Perez and his wife at their home in Racine, Wisconsin. By the time he accepted the CEO offer, Perez concluded that despite the differences in industry sector and corporate cultures, much of what he had learned over the years about marketing, management, and brands was indeed applicable to Nike. He also adopted the appropriate mind-set for someone moving into a leadership role from outside the organization. "I've got to learn from the Nike people and understand the culture," he said. "The last thing I want to do is disrupt it."

Well, despite the best of intentions and extensive due diligence on both sides, it did not work. Armed with the personal mandate from Knight to apply the sophisticated practices from packaged-goods marketing, one of Perez's early initiatives was to go out with members of the company's sales force to visit Nike's largest retail partners. This is Management 101 to those trained in the blue-chip consumer marketing world and exactly what Knight had hired Perez to do. Perhaps it was his reclusive personality or perhaps he didn't think it was necessary, but whatever the reason, Knight had not communicated his endorsement of Perez's new approach around the Beaverton, Oregon, campus. The new CEO seemed out of step, and the whispering campaign soon began. "*We* don't go out to visit the retailers and *sell* them our wares," longtime company managers said. "*They* come to us to *buy* our products." Such were the unwritten rules of how Nike had always done business. Executives were further taken aback when Perez sought to establish a consumer insights capability, using market research to understand what customers were looking for in Nike's offerings.

Again, for marketers at S. C. Johnson, Procter & Gamble, PepsiCo, or hundreds of other marketing-driven companies, forming such a group would have been considered a baby step toward linking product development with customer preferences. But not at Nike. "*We* don't ask consumers what they want," the way of thinking went. "We *design products* that they have never thought of and *show them* that they want them."[1]

Influential company executives started talking about how Perez didn't have an emotional connection to the Nike brand. He was too cold, overly numbers driven, and analytical. Long-serving executives started lining up outside Knight's Zen-garden-inspired office, from which he rarely ventured. "Perez just doesn't *get it*," they complained. "We're not selling Johnson's Wax here. We create the world's highest-performance footwear, apparel, and equipment for the greatest athletes on the planet whom our consumers strive to emulate." Behind closed doors Knight was being buffeted by these criticisms from trusted colleagues, many of whom had worked for Knight their entire careers. And while Knight and Perez had weekly meetings to review progress and priorities, the communications were breaking down between the two. Perez says that Knight had not given him feedback about the concerns coming to him from the executive team. Since he thought he was doing precisely what he had been hired to do, he was shocked when at the seemingly routine Monday meeting on January 9, 2006, only thirteen months after assuming the CEO position, Knight

---

1. Senior Nike executives are unapologetic about this approach, stressing correctly that other innovative companies such as Apple also *lead*—rather that react to—customer preferences.

delivered the fateful news. Perez told us what Knight said verbatim. "This is not working. You can resign amicably or go fight it with the board."

Perez did in fact appeal to the board, but to no avail. The irony is that Nike's performance during his short tenure was strong. Net income surged 28 percent to $1.2 billion from $950 million a year earlier, while sales rose 12 percent to $13.7 billion from $12.2 billion. The problem was clearly not one of performance. And contrary to the most common explanation, it was only partially a function of a cultural mismatch. Had the company been in a crisis situation, with a so-called burning platform for change, the initiatives that Perez was attempting to drive would have been more palatable and therefore almost certainly more successful. According to one senior Nike executive who was there at the time and who requested anonymity, "Bill's experience at Nike was doomed from the start. The belief from the outset was that the veterans would not stand for anyone from outside the company as CEO. There was a long history of a cabal of old-timers with Phil's ear who felt they could ignore Bill."

Mark Parker, the copresident of the Nike brand, was named CEO to replace Perez. Knight knew that Parker, who had been with the company for his entire working life, understood the essence of the Nike brand and that he would have the support of the top management team and broader organization. Evidently, for Nike at least, the so-called state-of-the-art marketing and sales techniques of focus-group-based product development, account management, and the like were not what the doctor ordered after all. While it may seem harsh to have replaced

Perez after such a short time as CEO, the fact is that many companies hesitate pulling the trigger to their detriment when things aren't working. Under Parker's understated but inspirational leadership and fit with the company's culture, history, and values, Nike has thrived through both economic boom and bust. Today, Nike continues to enjoy its reputation as one of the world's most innovative companies, with its Swoosh being one of the most recognized and valuable brands on the globe.

After the Nike debacle, Perez's formerly stellar career was in disarray. He received a number of calls about joining boards. But he turned them all down because he wanted to get back to work and was already on the Kellogg and Hallmark boards. He had "failed as a CEO" and had shown that "he couldn't adapt to another culture" after a lifetime inside the staid, private S. C. Johnson. Boards of directors, even in his very own consumer-products industry, were reticent to consider him for top executive positions. Perez was at a crossroads in his career, similar to many severed executives. Should he attempt to "get back up on the horse" and try to rebuild his reputation? Or should he slip into a comfortable retirement made possible by his lucrative Nike severance package?[2] *Surely* he had learned the lesson never again to work as an outsider CEO for a powerful chairman in a founder-led or family-controlled company.

Bill Perez and Bill Wrigley Jr., however, came to an altogether different conclusion. What next happened to Perez helps bring to light of day perhaps *the* essential truth when it comes to hiring a person for a top leadership job.

---

2. Perez's Nike severance, which was contractual, covered only about half of the amount of unvested long-term compensation when he departed S. C. Johnson.

It's not about selecting a great individual to do a job. It's about matching the *right* individual to the *right* situation, and using the *right* process to get it done.

That is our central message, one contrary to much that passes for conventional thinking used at most organizations when decisions are made about which people to place in senior-level positions. It's less about going out to find an individual superstar and more about deeply understanding what an organization needs and what kind of person would both fit into the culture and bring the right experience and skill set to get the job done and *then* going out to find the best person *to match* the need. While this may seem like common sense, we'll help you understand and internalize the fact that this is a different way of thinking about choosing the best person for the most important positions through compelling stories based on a wide variety of experiences and a multiyear internationally based research study. Our goal is to provide you with a framework and a process for using that framework when there is the need to fill key leadership positions not only at the top but throughout your organization.

WILLIAM WRIGLEY JR. II,[3] who stood at the helm of the company his great-grandfather founded in 1891, determined that he needed a seasoned executive to help navigate the company through the difficult absorption of the Altoids and Life Savers

---

3. Bill Jr. is the son of William Wrigley III (1933–1999), the grandson of Philip K. Wrigley (1894–1977), and the great-grandson of William Wrigley Jr. (1861–1932).

YOU NEED A LEADER—NOW WHAT?

businesses acquired from Kraft Foods for $1.5 billion in 2004. Wrigley suggested Perez as a candidate to the company's board based on his CEO experience at S. C. Johnson, where he had led the acquisition and integration of numerous consumer companies. Wrigley and the board conducted intensive due diligence on Perez's troubles at Nike and his extensive career at S. C. Johnson, speaking with board directors and former direct reports from both companies. Equally significantly, since Wrigley and S. C. Johnson shared many of the same retail customer accounts—including the largest supermarket chains, drugstores, and mass retailers—they were able to get an unbiased market point of view on Perez's reputation and management style. This research plus extensive conversations with Perez, during which he dispassionately shared his lessons learned from the Nike saga, helped Wrigley come to the conclusion that Perez's failure wasn't a question of him being "a bad" CEO. Also, Wrigley recognized that his company had more similarities to S. C. Johnson than to Nike in how it was managed, what processes it used in marketing, advertising, and product development, and how it sold into the retail channel. So they decided to go with Perez. When the Wm. Wrigley Jr. Company announced him as its new CEO on October 23, 2006, however, they confronted a number of challenges, including the baggage of Perez's negative Nike tenure and the fact that it was the first time that the Chicago company had ever gone outside the family, much less the company, for a new CEO.

The decision to appoint Perez was quickly validated inside the company, and soon thereafter in the marketplace and on Wall Street. Unlike Nike, where Knight had been mum about the changes that Perez was implementing, this time he had the visible and well-communicated support of chairman Bill Wrigley Jr. Perez was therefore able to immediately realign global operations to have all of the regions report directly to him. Also, he had the mandate to get directly involved in product development, engaging freely with the company's food scientists, flavoring experts, and manufacturing managers. Based on his past experience working with S. C. Johnson's sales force with grocery and convenience stores, he was able to relate to the Wrigley salespeople about how to win more shelf facings from the competition with the major retail customers. The result? Wrigley saw marked growth in international profits from a more efficient global supply chain. The product development teams revamped the flavors of their Extra and Wrigley's brands and spearheaded the introduction of the Slim Pack, a sleek, fifteen-stick envelope-style packaging that would be more durable and portable. Most significantly, with the support of market research and his prior new product development experience, Perez convinced the company's management team and board that their nine-figure investment in 5 Gum was worth it. The new packaging, marketing, and flavoring formulations unleashed unprecedented growth in the core chewing gum business in what was an otherwise mature industry.

In less than two years with Perez as CEO, Wrigley's share price increased by 50 percent, fueled by growth in revenues and net income of 23 percent and 29 percent, respectively. With Perez, the Wrigley Company was flourishing once again under the leadership of a CEO who came from the outside after three generations of family management. Perez's success as an externally recruited CEO at Wrigley defied much conventional wisdom about top management recruitment, such as: Don't select an executive who "failed"—since the decision would be received with skepticism by investors, the media, and even other managers—or based on widespread views that executives recruited from the outside are much riskier.

By October of 2008, the worldwide confectionery sector was following the path of many other industries in a seemingly inevitable march toward global consolidation. The industry giants—Kraft (which later acquired Cadbury), Nestlé, and Mars—were slugging it out for world dominance by competing to buy the smaller players and wrest operating efficiencies by integrating them into their global supply chains. Now that Wrigley had gone from a solid to star performer under Perez it became an irresistible acquisition target. So with the support of the Wrigley family and the company's board, Perez led the sale of Wrigley to Mars Inc. The $23 billion deal represented a 28 percent premium over the share price, and the sale was overwhelmingly approved by shareholders. In a less formal vote, the deal also won the approval of the company's management, who would stay in place as Wrigley became a stand-alone business unit of Mars. After the closing of the sale, Perez was able to leave the company, satisfied that it was in good hands and that his executive reputation was back intact.

The lesson?

It's not that Bill Perez was a "good" leader at Wrigley or a "bad" one at Nike that led to his success or failure. He had substantially the same directive at Nike and Wrigley. And he actually did many of the same things as CEO in both situations.

It turns out that it was really less about Perez the individual and more about Perez as a piece in distinctly different puzzles. At S. C. Johnson and Wrigley, Perez was the right fit. Even though he was the same person, the situational and cultural contexts were completely different at Nike, and that helps explain much of why the outcomes were dramatically different. Akin to scientists studying twins separated at birth to evaluate nature versus nurture, Bill Perez had the unique opportunity to serve as a private company CEO and then a public company CEO for two different companies in rapid succession. As a result, his experience is an illuminating example of how even an excellent manager will be successful only properly matched to the environment into which he is placed. If the piece does not fit nicely into the contextual jigsaw, all the talent, skills, and experience will be for naught or worse.

2. THE THREE ESSENTIAL TRUTHS FOR CHOOSING THE BEST PERSON FOR YOUR ORGANIZATION

D r. Jerome Barton, the senior orthopedic surgeon at the Norwalk, Connecticut, offices of Coastal Orthopaedics called asking for advice on how to recruit a new doctor to his practice. Four senior doctors had been partners for years, and it was time to bring in the next generation. There were a few problems. First, they hadn't found a way to agree on the ideal skill set. Should it be a hand, shoulder, or knee specialist? Or should it be a generalist? Second, they were terrified of bringing in a young doctor who had great credentials but who would turn out to be a bad fit with the cohesive and collaborative culture of the office. Third, how would they actually interview candidates to come to agreement and ensure the best result?

After some discussion, the approach became clear to Barton. He spent the weekend drafting a briefing document that would be both a road map as to what the four partners should be looking for and a selling document for prospective candidates. The paper provided background on the history of the practice, the key metrics of the office, the types of patients served, specialties covered, and the team-oriented structure and culture. Next, it articulated the desired professional experience (shoulder or knee specialty) and the interpersonal characteristics sought in candidates (collaboration, responsiveness, strong work ethic, positive disposition).

Then Barton sent the four-page document to his partners and suggested they discuss it in the office on Monday morning. With the first draft of the "spec" in hand, it made for a constructive and relatively even-keeled conversation and they quickly achieved consensus on what they were looking for. Later, the finalized document was sent to each of the candidates in advance of their interviews. None of these up-and-coming doctors had ever seen any other medical practice be so strategic in their hiring, which presented Coastal in a positive and highly differentiated light. When it came to the interviews, rather than having relatively unstructured conversations with variability from one candidate to another, Barton and his partners developed specific questions linked to the requirements to ask each candidate. They also agreed to interview as a group so that they would all experience the candidates in the same way, and while one partner was asking questions, the others could listen. This had the additional benefit of bringing to life the collaborative and cohesive culture that was so important at Coastal. After each interview, they spent fifteen minutes comparing notes about what they liked and didn't like about the candidate. Finally, at the end of the long day, the four doctors completed a rating sheet scoring each candidate on the specific professional and personal attributes listed in the spec. After about an hour of discussion, presenting and defending various candidates and scores, a unanimous choice emerged. Their top choice was hired, and in the time since he started he has brought a new energy and positive dynamic to their practice.

The thought process and approach of *You Need a Leader—Now What?* helped four highly experienced doctors come to agreement on what they were looking for and how to pursue it. As a result, they successfully solved a succession decision that could otherwise have been emotion charged and risky.

Now think, on average, how many people decisions do *you* make a day? Decisions such as: Who is the right person for the job? Who is the best colleague to lead a work group? To whom should I assign a particular project? Whose judgment do I trust with a sensitive piece of information?

At least five, no matter whether you work in a corporation, not-for-profit, consulting firm, bank, health-care facility, or school. That means about one thousand people-related decisions over the course of the year, not including weekends, evenings, or vacations when you may also be deciding who should head up the parents' committee at school, whom to hire to plan the wedding, or whom to entrust with your finances.

People decisions—especially those involving leadership jobs—have exponential consequences on both the upside and downside; and the more senior the leadership appointment, the greater the ramifications. When you get these decisions right, you achieve better results and do so with much less time and angst. You lead a more satisfying and balanced day-to-day life because you attract better people who work more independently and produce better results. The most important work gets done well and in a timely fashion. It is even better when these are people whom you both respect and enjoy spending time with. You create and reinforce a culture in which you and your colleagues can do your best work and you unleash a virtuous cycle in which strong performers attract other strong performers and good performance leads to better performance.

On the other side of the coin, getting it wrong can land you in a quagmire. When your employees are weak, you are forced to spend more time and emotional energy explaining what needs to get done and how to do it. You'll soon be looking in the mirror and seeing that micromanager you've always detested and resented. Choosing the wrong people forces you to spend more time adjudicating issues that others should be capable of resolving. That client report that you were counting on doesn't meet your standards and you find yourself having to send it back or, more likely, redoing the work yourself. Project teams turn dysfunctional and argumentative rather than vehicles for getting things done.

> Whether you are involved in helping to recruit a new corporate chief executive, selecting the next president of a museum, or hiring any senior manager, there is a core set of three principles—essential truths—about what to do, how to do it, and what not to do. Applied together they will dramatically improve your rate of success in making important people leadership decisions.

We believe that the lessons of *You Need a Leader—Now What?* will also help guide you in your own professional career. When you have the opportunity to consider your next job, you will have greater insight into how decisions are made at the highest levels, which will in turn help you get the positions you want and support you in achieving your goals.

The spark for our book came from a conversation we had in the summer of 2008 with people from a financial services firm involved in the search for a new chief executive. There were two internal candidates we were asked to assess for their readiness to take on the top job. Simultaneously we did a benchmarking exercise to identify the best industry talent outside the company and then compared them to the two internal people under consideration. When the chairman of the board asked for our assessment of the insiders versus the outsiders, we told her, "You have two strong internal candidates, one marginally stronger relative to the future challenges of the company. While there are several attractive external potential candidates who would be viable and attractable, our judgment is that on a risk-adjusted basis it is a better bet to promote from within."

The part of the comment that most caught the chairman's attention was "on a risk-adjusted basis." She asked us to present this assessment to the full board, and during that meeting we discussed the findings from our work—assessments of the two internal candidates, one slightly better than the other, profiles and performance analyses of ten top industry executives, and our recommendation to stay inside for the next CEO. When we repeated the line that so captivated the chairman, one of the directors asked a question that in one moment seemed to cut to the very core of our professional experience. "How do you *know*," he asked, "when it's worth the risk of going outside for new leadership?"

We responded with a touch more confidence than was justified. "When a company like yours has a clear strategic direction, is in good financial condition, and you have a strong internal candidate," we said, "there is a much greater likelihood of success staying inside rather than risking the organ rejection of going outside." This certainly met the logic test, and the probing director seemed satisfied. But the question "How do you know?" was one we continued to think about. The answer we gave was based on many years of experiences in industries ranging from high technology, consumer products, and banking to media, hospitality, and automotive. But it was not drawn from empirical evidence, and that distinction bothered us. The more we thought about it, the more evident it became that the data were there ready to be analyzed. What, in fact, *was* the history of success for organizations staying inside versus going outside for new leadership? When did it work and why? Under what circumstances did it blow up? Did the answer differ between for-profit companies and not-for-profit institutions? Did it vary by industry, point in the economic cycle, company size, or the background or experience of the new leader? Answers to these questions would increase the odds of success in making the most important people leadership decisions.

So we embarked on an eighteen-month research project to study leadership transitions. It not only became the basis of this book, but changed how we conduct our most important CEO search and succession planning engagements.

The study initially focused on what worked best and worst in CEO transitions in the United States. It was a rigorous performance analysis of CEO transitions for large public companies in the United States, the S&P 500. We then expanded it to address smaller companies in the Russell 2000 Index. We also went beyond the corporate world to analyze leadership transitions at the top thirty research universities in the United States as well as leading liberal arts colleges, major museums, and other cultural institutions. The research then moved beyond the United States to analyze CEO transitions among the major companies in France, Germany, the Netherlands, and the United Kingdom.

The insights from this research are not only directly applicable to selecting new leaders for the very top job, but they can be used for making a wide range of key people decisions across the organization and in everyday life. The study findings can become the foundation for developing a framework that is based on both art and science, combining your intuition based on years of personal experience, with analysis. Your gut-level instincts as to whether someone is—or is not—a good fit can be backed up by research-based principles and best practices. It can ground your process in a forward-looking approach of where your organization is headed, a rigorous internal and external assessment, and a high level of involvement by key constituencies. Your decisions can be made so that they take advantage of the experiences of similar organizations, some of which have stayed internal and others that have gone outside, and the conditions that correlate with success and failure in each case. You can establish based on your situation, a customized, two-track approach—one internal and one external—that comes together at decision time as to who is the best leader for your situation at that point in time.

This research-powered two-track leadership selection process works and has been used by a wide range of organizations in diverse industries and contexts: the world's largest technology company dealing with the forced removal of its chief executive, a $50 billion global financial institution having just completed a landmark acquisition necessitating vastly different leadership skills, a $3 billion global hotel company and a $5 billion retailer going through successions when their top executives were removed for performance reasons, a $7 billion cable television company and a world-renowned library conducting orderly successions due to the retirement of high-performing long-serving leaders, and a public broadcasting organization and school system engaging their broad community of stakeholders in new ways to determine their future direction. It has even been used by the board of a New York City co-op apartment building in the selection of a new superintendent and in the orthopedic medical group mentioned earlier. The jobs have ranged from chief financial officers to heads of human resources and chief marketing officers using an approach based on understanding and applying the three essential truths of leadership selection:

1. It's not about finding a "great" individual; it's about solving an intricate and dynamic jigsaw puzzle.

2. Once you have diagnosed the need, then you can get the very best person.

3. Even the right choice can go wrong without the right process.

ESSENTIAL TRUTH #1: IT'S NOT ABOUT FINDING A "GREAT" INDIVIDUAL; IT'S ABOUT SOLVING AN INTRICATE AND DYNAMIC JIGSAW PUZZLE

When you're selecting someone to take on a key leadership position or making any important people decision, rather than thinking about it as "filling a hole," which is a static concept with a singular need and individual solution, recognize that you're hiring that person into a system, a vibrant and dynamic puzzle. No one works in a vacuum. The best business leaders have great teams and throughout their careers have generated strong followership. In today's world of information transparency, knowledge and attitudes also spread immediately so an organization is more likely to embrace *or reject* someone in a new position much more rapidly than in the past. Just look at the venerable publishing company Time Inc. After two decades of stable leadership under CEOs Don Logan and Ann Moore, respectively, a new CEO recruited from the outside, Jack Griffin, was removed after a mere five months in the job. The reason? He did not fit. While Griffin was previously the highly regarded president of Meredith Corporation's national media group, where he successfully expanded the company's magazine titles and created sophisticated integrated marketing programs for clients, it took only a matter of months for employees and executives alike to conclude that Griffin's brusque management style was out of sync with the Time Inc. corporate culture. The internal memorandum sent to company staff by Jeff Bewkes, chief executive of Time Inc. parent company

Time Warner, explained the decision with clarity often too rare in corporate circles: "I regret to inform you that Jack Griffin is leaving his position as Chairman and CEO of Time Inc. Although Jack is an extremely accomplished executive, I concluded that his leadership style and approach did not mesh with Time Inc. and Time Warner."

Companies—any organized group of people for that matter—have always operated through both formal organization charts and unwritten rules of "the way things are done around here." If you actually trace how decisions are made, how work gets done, and how problems are solved, it will be clear that some people are opinion makers; and regardless of where they sit on the organization chart, their views can sway others. This is how a dynamic organizational system works in real life. Whether it has to do with hiring a person or working on any project, the best managers responsible for the task will seek out the opinions of these key influencers. When the influencers give their support, the unofficial organization kicks in. People reach out to their trusted colleagues to determine what to make of the new person or priority and subsequently decide whether or not to lend their support. Once their decision is made, they may smile and say yes to your face, but if they have come up on the side against your approach, they will find ways to undermine the effort.

One new CEO learned this the hard way, eventually figuring out why several of his top priorities weren't gaining any traction. There were organizational blockers who said yes to a new priority, and gave a thumbs-up with a cheerful demeanor, but who assumed they would outlast the new leader. As a result, they went back to the way they *really* got things done around there. When the new CEO finally figured out what was happening, he terminated the most egregiously offending executive. The CEO then found two well-respected but formerly blocked managers who were enthusiastic about the new direction and things finally started to move. Success is often achieved like this, when a leader fits into, and gels with, all of the other pieces of the system and he has developed an effective means of working with and through others. At this point when decisions are broadly supported and shared across the organization, things get done.

To use the metaphor of round pegs and square holes is to miss the point of the dynamic puzzle. It's not just one hole that needs to be filled with a good fit. It's about understanding the broader set of constituencies that will have an influence on whether or not the appointment takes hold—and then solving for that by understanding what each person or group is looking for and involving them in the process in the right way. To illustrate, we will look at the process used by one of the world's most important not-for-profit organizations, the New York Public Library, when recruiting a new president (pages 33–43).

ESSENTIAL TRUTH #2: ONCE YOU HAVE DIAGNOSED THE NEED, THEN YOU CAN GET THE VERY BEST PERSON

Once you accurately diagnose what is needed to solve the organizational puzzle, then you actually have to identify, choose, and attract the very best person to fit into this situation. Sometimes the best person for the job may have actually less experience than others. Yet, as we illustrate in the case of appointing a first-timer at Starwood Hotels & Resorts Worldwide, there are conditions when this is the right decision.

We will then provide insights from our CEO Transition Study to provide an empirical foundation for this second essential truth of how to find the best person for an important leadership role. Different situations and varied scenarios will be explored to guide you in determining who the right person is for the organization at a particular point in time, such as when to promote from within and when to recruit from the outside.

When deciding on the best person for a key role, you are likely to be swayed by long-held assumptions about what makes the right choice. In fact, this so-called conventional wisdom frequently influences hiring managers and boards of directors. Just as important as helping you understand what to bring into your people leadership decisions, we will also shed light on those factors that turn out to be unimportant at best, misdirected at worst, in predicting performance. These "red herrings" have to do with commonly held but often misplaced notions about hiring people of a particular age, set of experience, or ethnicity.

ESSENTIAL TRUTH #3: EVEN THE RIGHT CHOICE CAN GO WRONG WITHOUT THE RIGHT PROCESS

Everyone knows that process is as boring as it is important, and yet boards of directors, trustees, search committees, and hiring managers that have their acts together and follow the right process can become magnets for talent. Even an organization in trouble can attract an A-player into a top leadership post. The key is projecting a realistic assessment of the situation, having the right aspirations, and ensuring a unified commitment and communication of those aspirations, evidenced by the alignment of key constituencies behind the person hired. Conversely, even a great business or institution can repel top talent if the hiring team is dysfunctional or the hiring process is flawed. It is therefore essential to follow the right process in order to get the leadership selection right.

It is all too common to look only at success stories and assert a causal link. It is, however, often equally instructive to delve into cases that went awry, even despite the most admirable of objectives, and draw lessons learned. To underscore the importance of correctly diagnosing the situation and then making the right choice, especially in a top leadership selection, we will show the dramatic consequences of landing off the mark through one of the most iconic companies in the world, and the boom-and-bust story of its CEO (pages 119–128).

We will demonstrate how constituency interviews can set you and the next leader up for success (pages 129–136). We'll then consider the risks and rewards of establishing a horse race to select a new leader and show how to orchestrate candidate interviews (pages 137–152). Then we will put it all together into what we believe is the very best practice in leadership selection by illustrating the actual succession process of a multibillion-dollar company, to which we have given the pseudonym "Major Global Incorporated" (pages 155–183).

We will then identify the most common pitfalls in leadership selection. For instance, we will show how easy—and how costly—it is to fall into the traps of hiring based on charisma, or not wanting anyone who has experienced a failure, or short-cutting the process due to time constraints (pages 192–206). We will also explore the seemingly logical succession process of a two-step appointment (i.e., bringing in a number two and, when he or she is "ready," making the promotion into the top job), and show why it can be a formula for failure (pages 206–212).

Finally, we will step out of the realm of the CEO, boards of directors, and top executive positions and take aim at how to apply the lessons from *You Need a Leader—Now What?* in everyday decision making across any organization or group of people. You might be surprised to see how widely the approach can be applied, from hiring the superintendent of an apartment building to bringing on new trustees to the board of a liberal arts college.

II.
SOLVE THE ORGANIZATIONAL JIGSAW PUZZLE

3. *PATIENCE* AND *FORTITUDE*: THE NEW YORK PUBLIC LIBRARY PRESIDENTIAL SEARCH

itting majestically astride the steps on Manhattan's Fifth Avenue at Forty-Second Street are *Patience* and *Fortitude,* the giant marble lions that have framed visitors' entry to the New York Public Library since the dedication of the Beaux-Arts building on May 23, 1911. *Patience* sits on the south side of the library's steps, and *Fortitude* guards the north. They were given their names in the 1930s by Mayor Fiorello LaGuardia as a way to stress the qualities he felt New Yorkers would need to survive the Great Depression. Both inviting and just a little menacing, *Patience* and *Fortitude* serve as the icon and logo of the library. But they may just as well have served as an *aide memoire* to the board of trustees when they set out to select a new president for this important and complex institution.

Not unlike the library itself, lions as a species are proud, serious, beautiful, and intimidating. They live in prides that are difficult for an outsider to break into. All of these descriptors were just as apt for the individuals who would be potential presidential candidates and the board who would be considering them. The New York Public Library, popularly known as NYPL, is a complex not-for-profit organization facing the pressures of rapidly changing technologies; economic forces and demographics; a diverse range of constituents all passionate

33

about the mission of the library; and a unique public- and private-sector business model. Taken all together, these various factors and workings create a jigsaw-like puzzle. If they were going to choose the right leader, those on the board's search committee had to recognize this and then consider candidates who would not just fit in at NYPL, but fit *into* its dynamic system. Likewise, the candidates would have to be aware of the interdependent complexities if they were going to be successful. How NYPL went about choosing its new president serves as an instructive example of the way the pieces of a complicated jigsaw puzzle work when it comes to selecting a key leader.

THE NYPL WAS created in 1895 through the consolidation of the private libraries of John Jacob Astor and James Lenox with the Samuel Jones Tilden Trust. Today, NYPL is one of the few institutions with both world-class research and circulating collections that are free and open to the general public. The library's deeply democratic mission goes back to its founding when it became a vital part of the intellectual fabric of New York City. It provided support for the waves of newly arrived immigrants and gave them a place to learn the English language and gain access to education, entertainment, and culture, all at no cost. This same offering resonates just as loudly with today's users. In 2010, the library had over eighteen million in-person visits plus an additional twenty-nine million visits to its website, NYPL.org. Sitting atop seven floors of book stacks, the library's enormous Deborah, Jonathan F. P., Samuel Priest, and Adam R. Rose Main Reading Room is one of the most exquisite public spaces in New York City and provides an inspirational learning space for tens of thousands of readers over the course of a year.

The board's task was to find the right person to succeed seventeen-year president Paul LeClerc. It is always challenging to recruit a successor to a long-serving and high-performing leader, which LeClerc most certainly was. Under his watch, the library experienced a tripling of in-person visits since 1993, acquired and preserved new collections (including the archives of Jack Kerouac, Jerome Robbins, and Malcolm X), and established partnerships with Google, Sony, and iTunes. Despite these successes, NYPL was at a significant crossroads, and there were four factors that taken together made this presidential search especially tricky.

First was finding a leader who both understood and could take action to address the daunting demands and opportunities posed by the advances of digital technology and the rapidly changing world of information creation and consumption. Ask many teenagers the last time they went to the library to find a book or do research and they'll give you one of those patronizing looks about how out of touch you are. So part of the challenge was keeping the library relevant to an up-and-coming generation that sees it as largely irrelevant. Second was to find someone who could raise enough money for the library to continue providing the highest-quality service to savvy twenty-first-century users, free of charge. NYPL depends on philanthropy and New York City and State funding for its sources of revenue—not user fees. So the new president would have to be skilled at motivating philanthropists whacked by the economic crisis to give and be effective at protecting the library's position as a top priority for funding in a budget-starved city and state. Third was doing this within a proud and often change-resistant organization. Just as companies around the world had to develop their customer service skills, solving problems over the phone and online, so too did the library need to develop its user support skills and transform itself from being an information repository to becoming one part live search engine and one part computer help desk. Fourth and finally was meeting the towering standards of a board comprising a who's who of New York society and some of America's foremost business leaders and scholars. NYPL trustees included the CEOs of major New York City–based corporations and several of the largest private equity firms in the world, heads of some of the world's most

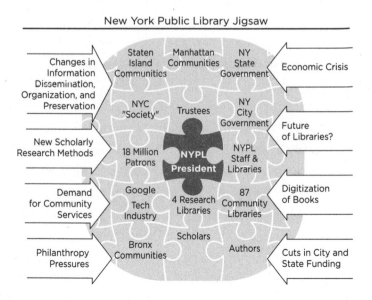

New York Public Library Jigsaw

prestigious foundations, and leading authors, professors, and patrons of the arts.

The new president would have to fit into this complex puzzle and engage effectively with all of these pieces. The majority of the library's funding is generated through philanthropy. Since the trustees and other major individual donors provide a disproportionately large share of revenue, they are therefore an essential constituency, and their views about the direction of NYPL and the leadership requirements for the next president were especially important. Through private meetings with trustees, both in individual and group settings, it became clear how important it was that the new president be an inspiring visionary who could paint a compelling picture of the role of libraries in the future and in so doing be effective interacting with and raising money from some of the most prominent private citizens in the world. The NYPL president had to be skilled at entertaining and being entertained in a sophisticated New York City social milieu populated by society mavens. But since funding does not come from private sources alone, the library must vie with other cultural and educational institutions to compete for increasingly scarce public funding from New York City and State. Thus, a core presidential skill is to lobby and sell the NYPL case to city council members, budgetary authorities, and other experienced players in the hardball game of New York City politics. On top of this, city and state funding decisions are also a function of trusted personal relationships, which means that in addition to everything else, the president must be willing to show up at the weddings, funerals, and other

personal and professional events of government leaders across
New York.

Trustees and staff alike take NYPL's mission very seriously.
They speak about the library as homage to democracy, a sancti-
fied and ecumenical place. One needs no documents to enter.
You will never be asked for an ID. It is a militant defender of
privacy. Librarians view themselves on the front lines of defending the Constitution and believe deeply in the rights of the
citizenry to libraries. Many New Yorkers cannot imagine the
city without the library.

The New York Public Library is essentially two separate institutions, each with distinct missions, delivery systems, cultures, and constituencies. On the one hand, NYPL is a great
research library considered by scholars to be both a source
of knowledge and a vehicle for generating new knowledge. It
boasts 50 million items in its collection, of which 14.5 million
are books and resources that include some of the most venerable artifacts of human culture, such as the copy of the Dec-
laration of Independence written in Thomas Jefferson's own
hand and a copy of the Gutenberg Bible. It also holds the literary papers of many important American and British authors,
genealogical records, thousands of maps and atlases from the
sixteenth century to the present, one of the world's great collections of Judaica materials, a fine arts research collection,
and an extensive trove of photographic images. On the other
hand, NYPL is very much what its name suggests—a public
library with a huge branch system in Manhattan, the Bronx,
and Staten Island (the Brooklyn and Queens public libraries
are separate institutions) serving millions of users each year.

The branch libraries serve as centers in their communities for education, enrichment, access to technology, after-school programs, and job-search support.

The new president therefore would need to excel in all areas of not-for-profit leadership, including generating financial support from New York's city and state governments and corporate and private donors, as well as having the intellectual and scholarly credibility to inspire research scholars and professional librarians. He or she would also need to have the strategic, people, and technology skills to lead the library successfully through a dramatically changing landscape.

The process of researching, developing and assessing prospective candidates took several months before the initial slate of candidates was ready for the search committee to interview. The committee reviewed the backgrounds of over two hundred prospects (ideas generated through proactive research and nominations) from the top academic institutions, leading libraries around the world, cultural institutions, diversified media conglomerates, and prominent Internet companies. With the jigsaw puzzle squarely in mind, the list was winnowed down to twenty-five individuals with whom discussions were had by telephone. Based on these conversations, which both furthered the committee's understanding of the prospective candidates' backgrounds and probed their potential interest levels, the committee was able to determine who were the most compelling. The final slate of candidates who were interviewed in person ultimately came from both the not-for-profit and corporate sectors, one-third of whom were women and one-fifth of whom were racially diverse.

The committee also spent time in varied settings with the finalists getting to know them as real people rather than just candidates interviewing for a job. Over lunches, discussions took place about technology vision and fund-raising strategies, and in private dinners at the home of trustees' Park Avenue apartments, leadership and management styles were probed. Before the ultimate decision was made as to the person who was their first choice candidate, the cochairs of the search committee spent a full day visiting the college where he was president and were able to see him on his home turf and experience his interactions with the campus community. Finally, with all the interviews, references, meals, visits, and compensation negotiations completed, it was announced on October 6, 2010, that Dr. Anthony W. (Tony) Marx, president of Amherst College and a distinguished political scientist, would become the library's next president and CEO, effective July 2011.

Why was Marx determined to be the right leader to fit the challenging situation of NYPL and how does his selection illustrate the concept of solving a complex jigsaw puzzle as the first essential truth in leadership selection? To begin with, Marx has a strong personal connection with NYPL. A native New Yorker, he attended Public School 98 and the Bronx High School of Science. As a child, he spent after-school hours studying and reading at his neighborhood Inwood branch, near the northern tip of Manhattan. His educational journey took him from the New York City public schools to an undergraduate career at Wesleyan University and Yale, then on to Africa in his twenties. He helped found Khanya College, a South African secondary school that prepared more than a thousand black students for university. Later, at Princeton University he earned a master's degree from the Woodrow Wilson School in 1987 and a PhD in politics in 1990. Next he spent thirteen years at Columbia University as a professor and then director of undergraduate studies in political science. He subsequently became the youngest president in Amherst College's history when he assumed the post in 2003. Over his eight years leading Amherst, Marx earned wide recognition for his passionate promotion of socioeconomic diversity and accessibility to higher education for lower-income students.

Of course, not only does the person have to be the right fit for an organization, but the position has to make sense for him as well. Marx not only was attracted to the library so he could return to his hometown (and rejoin his wife who is a tenured professor at Columbia), but also was motivated to take his experience, skills, and interests and apply them in a new and important venue. "The New York Public Library unites the world of advanced scholarship and the world of universal education," Marx said when he accepted the position. "It conserves our cultural heritage and pushes ahead into new technological and intellectual frontiers. It cherishes both the tranquillity of the reading room and the vocal debates of the public square. It is 'local' in the sense that New York is local—a community with global implications."

An accomplished scholar, Marx brought an appreciation for the demands and nuances of research. As Amherst's president, Marx also proved himself to be a capable manager, strong community builder, and highly effective fund-raiser. "Tony's ideals are matched by his prolific fund-raising ability," commented

Jide Zeitlin, chairman of the Amherst board of trustees. "Successfully leading the largest campaign in the history of Amherst College, he set fund-raising records enabling the college's remarkable progress." During Marx's tenure as president, Amherst received the two largest gifts in the history of the college and the largest unrestricted gift to *any* liberal arts college.

Perhaps the single most important achievement that made Marx the candidate of choice for the NYPL search committee was his track record providing underrepresented groups equal access to educational opportunities. As Amherst's president, he addressed growing class divisions and constriction in economic and social mobility through improved access. By championing increased socioeconomic diversity and consistently maintaining Amherst's position as a leading undergraduate institution, he was credited with transforming the college. From a technological perspective, Marx made it a priority to leverage information technology to enhance Amherst's institutional research, improve teaching and pedagogy, build better platforms for student advising and registration, and connect students and alumni in new and creative ways. Nevertheless, leadership selection is always about making trade-offs—there is never a *perfect* candidate—and even though Marx had dealt with the challenges of IT, it was the one area where he was lighter in expertise than other finalist candidates. The search committee and Marx himself recognized that there would be some work to bring him up to speed on the latest digital technologies and how they would need to be leveraged to help confront the transformational challenges facing the library. One criterion that could not be taught or studied, on the other hand, is an intuitive understanding of the city in which NYPL plays such an important role. As a native New Yorker, Marx has a nuanced understanding of New York City that will enable him to be an effective partner with city governmental and community leaders. Finally, in everything he has done over the course of his life and career, Marx has demonstrated a passionate commitment to the fundamental purpose of the New York Public Library: to inspire learning, advance knowledge, and strengthen communities.

Tony Marx's selection as president and CEO of NYPL is a rich example of the importance of looking at your organization as a complex and interdependent system. The rigor that the search committee applied in understanding the key constituencies and their stated and unstated interests; the forces at work confronting the institution internally and externally; and the strategic, economic, organizational, and cultural situation at play enabled the committee members to bring on board an individual who they believe is the right leader to fit their particular circumstances at this point in time and, they hope, well into the future.

III.
CHOOSE THE VERY BEST PERSON ONCE YOU'VE DIAGNOSED THE NEED

4. THE APPOINTMENT OF A FIRST-TIMER

In April 2007, Starwood Hotels & Resorts Worldwide, one of the world's largest hotel companies, with such brands as Westin, St. Regis, Sheraton, and W, initiated a search for its next CEO. The stakes were especially high since Starwood's former leader had departed after culture clashes and management missteps. Organizational morale had been damaged and a leadership vacuum exposed the company to competitive incursion from aggressive rivals such as Marriott, Hyatt, and Hilton. These established competitors and up-and-coming boutique hotel companies, such as Morgans Hotels, were also targeting Starwood's top management talent and one-hundred-thousand-plus associates.

Frits van Paasschen was the person recommended to the board of directors by the search committee. He was CEO of Coors Brewing Company (a division of corporate parent Molson Coors Brewing Company) and had public company board experience as a director of sunglasses and sports equipment maker Oakley and retail company Jones Apparel Group. At Coors, van Paasschen had full responsibility for a $2.6 billion business, an organization of forty-five hundred employees, over five hundred independent distributors, and the world's largest brewery and aluminum can plant. He led a reversal of a years-long decline in market share by reaching out to distributors, introducing packaging innovation, such as the aluminum can with lettering that turned blue when cold (to reinforce the marketing message of ice cold beer from the Rocky Mountains), and instilling operational excellence across the business. The distributor experience was relevant to hotel owners, and innovation remains a cornerstone for Starwood's brands. He had a stellar prior career at Nike in Asia and Europe, where over a four-year period he led the company's growth—the vast majority of which was organic—of over 60 percent from $2.5 billion to $4 billion and also doubled operating profits to $800 million. His earlier experience was at Disney (in strategic planning and consumer products) and at McKinsey & Company. Starwood's board unanimously approved the decision, even though van Paasschen lacked the public company CEO experience of the two other finalist candidates. The members of the committee carefully weighed the value of proven public company CEO experience versus the potential of a candidate who would be a first-time CEO but who would bring relevant multi-industry, international, marketing-oriented general management experience; operational expertise; and analogous client relations experience with bottlers that bore similarity to hotel owners. He would bring one other thing that the two other finalists could not—a passion and energy level that is often present when someone is on the cusp of gaining the top job for the first time.

It raised a vexing question that often comes up in making leadership decisions. When does the value of potential outweigh the value of experience?

For a company to put its trust, fiduciary responsibilities, and reputation behind a new leader, it is largely a game of confidence. Once they have selected a new CEO, the members of the board of directors will leave the room and go back to their own day-to-day pressure-packed lives until the next board meeting. They will be passing the baton of responsibility to the new leader to carry the company forward in a way that they can feel secure about. Boards are therefore looking for someone who both understands the situation in a deep way and who can develop a specific plan of action for leading the organization through the maze of issues and opportunities to optimize short-term and long-term results. Those factors that contribute to a candidate engendering confidence are intellectual prowess; the ability to articulate a point of view in a clear and compelling way; a strong values match between the individual, the directors, and the company; and finally, executive presence—that intangible ability to inspire confidence in a group setting. Through multiple rounds of interviews, it became clear that van Paasschen had all of these things. But the qualities that really separated him from the other finalists, the capabilities that underlay these essential attributes and tied them all together, were his ability to think clearly and communicate effectively.

There was a wide divergence among the Starwood CEO candidates along the dimension of clarity of thinking. In van Paasschen's case, he had a well-founded point of view and was able to stake out a position that made sense with conviction. He demonstrated the ability to deal with complex issues in a straightforward manner and to provide clear analysis. Specifically, he was best able to explain the key competitive dynamics in the global hospitality industry (i.e., what was driving change, what new brands and hotel formats were on the ascendancy, and who was losing and why) and coherently describe what Starwood should do to thrive (i.e., what the top priorities should be, what strategies should be pursued, and what acquisitions should be considered). He was also able to present a sound and detailed organizational architecture that in his view would enable the company to execute the strategy most effectively—that is, how he would structure the company along geographic and functional axes, what positions should report directly to the CEO, which functions should be centralized and which pushed into the business divisions, and how to align incentive systems to reward the desired behaviors.

The less successful candidates, those who did not make the short list, were by stark contrast muddled in their thinking, unclear about the company's priorities, generic about what strategies to pursue, and generally all over the place as to how they would make necessary changes in the structure of the company to respond to a changing marketplace. One component of the process that the Starwood search committee deployed in order to choose among the three finalist candidates was an executive intelligence assessment. A specialized executive assessment consultant interviewed each finalist and presented four real-life business scenarios, asking how each candidate would make decisions and manage through them. These dynamic discussions and the various responses were compared to those of thousands of other top executives who had been assessed through these same cases. Van Paasschen scored in the top five percentile among all respondents in the measurement of the cognitive skills that correlate to top leadership success. The quantitative and qualitative information produced by the executive assessment process, combined with more traditional competency-based interviewing and detailed references, provides information and insights that are the most accurate predictor of leadership success; van Paasschen stacked up exceptionally well.

One of the final steps in the Starwood search process was asking the finalist candidates to develop written plans for their first hundred days as CEO if they were selected. Van Paasschen's plan was ambitious and confidence inspiring—the embodiment of his clear, coherent, and critical thinking skills. It laid out a specific and exciting road map for the company under his leadership. In early 2011, upon revisiting his memo, van Paasschen commented to us, "I chuckle at how ambitious the plan is. It is impossible to get this much done in 100 days. Yet I'm struck by how relevant it is still today. The first 100 days should be about making as much progress as possible and laying the foundation for more work. By the way, identifying and parsing key strategic issues is a lot easier than addressing and solving them!"

MEMORANDUM

To: Members of the Starwood Board of Directors

From: Frits van Paasschen

Date: July 2007

Subject: My First 100 Days as CEO

INTRODUCTION

The purpose of this document is to provide an outline of what I plan to accomplish during my first 100 days as the new CEO of Starwood. I would welcome any and all input from the Board into this plan. At the same time, it contains what I see as "must haves" to build credibility with key stakeholders while ensuring the growth and prosperity of the company.

I will focus on five objectives during my first 100 days. These priorities also form the structure of this document.

I. Validate the strategy.

II. Lay the foundation for aligning the top team with each other and with our strategy.

III. Begin communications with key stakeholders: employees, franchisees/owners, customers, investment community, and the Board.

IV. Develop an initial perspective on the organizational structure.

V. Understand the key financial and operational levers in managing the company.

Above all, I intend to build a personal, independent view of where Starwood is today—strategically, organizationally, and financially. The goal is to identify immediate needs of the company while building the needed alignment and relationships to ensure success in my new role.

I. VALIDATE THE STRATEGY

Why focus on strategy? Getting the company aligned and focused follows from having a clear strategy which is not only understood but also provides a touchstone for guiding actions, organizational structure, allocating time and money, and monitoring performance. For me, it is literally the framework that I use to lead.

To start, it is useful to summarize the strategy in 5 simple, declarative sentences. These strategies can then: 1) be fleshed out in more detail, 2) serve as the framework for planning and action throughout the company, and 3) be made tangible and specific by having performance measures and milestones attached to them. The acid test of whether a company is being strategically led is whether front-line employees—all employees, for that matter—believe they play a role in realizing the strategy.

I choose the words "validate the strategy" because the company is performing well (in the marketplace and in terms of shareholder value), the investment community is supportive of the direction, and the Board has endorsed the strategy. Still, it is important for the CEO to evaluate the strategy critically, embrace it, and, most importantly, find out what it will take to drive it forward.

To be sure, the plan is not to resolve and define every aspect of the strategy during the first 100 days. However, any unresolved or undefined elements of the strategy should be clearly identified. By the same token, I expect that many, if not most, of the strategic questions will already have been addressed by the organization.

Here is a preliminary view of the 5 strategic priorities:

1) Grow through brand strength by executing tailored strategies for each brand

2) Align operations to support each brand strategy

3) Optimize the real-estate portfolio ("asset light")

4) Lead global consolidation

5) Pursue growth opportunities through new businesses

Beyond these five basic strategies, there are other issues that warrant being incorporated into the overall strategy. It may be important, for example, to focus on reducing corporate costs, particularly in White Plains (total SG&A has increased considerably in the past couple of years). This would take place in tandem with reviewing organizational structure and identifying whether there are duplicated functions, or ones to be outsourced, decentralized, or moved offshore. Benchmarks of overhead costs might also be useful.

Another important area is Corporate and Social Responsibility (CSR). Increasingly, consumers care as much about the brands they buy as the companies behind those brands. I believe there is an opportunity to build brand loyalty by credibly leading and driving innovation in CSR. These efforts could also be discreetly brought to life for guests during their stay.

The CSR agenda would address environmental impact (e.g., EPA Climate Savers), diversity, and corporate philanthropy. In each case, the key is to make the efforts integrated with the business operations, cost effective, and brand consistent.

II. LAY THE FOUNDATION FOR ALIGNING THE TOP TEAM

Critical also in the first 100 days is getting smart about the alignment, commitment, and ability of the top team (the CEO's direct reports, plus a few other critical positions). Key issues to probe:

- Are top team members aligned with the strategy?

- Do they trust one another and work well together?

- Is there a healthy rhythm and structure to communications?

- Is decision-making fact-based and "boundary-less"?

- Are all top team members focused on the same measures of success?

- Are there any gaps in the team that need to be immediately addressed (such as initiating a search for a global head of HR or CMO)? Does there need to be a head of pricing?

One step in aligning the top team will involve one-on-one meetings focused on issues such as: professional and personal goals, perspectives on the business and strategy, and perceptions of top team dynamics. Also important will be finding the right way to meet as a team and drive through an agenda.

When joining Coors Brewing Company as a new CEO, I found it useful to probe similar issues in group and 1x1 meetings with the direct the reports of the top team ("skip level" meetings).

III. LAUNCH COMMUNICATIONS

With a CEO transition, it will be important to build confidence among many constituencies that have interests in the company. My personal communication style is open, direct, and generally informal. Below are four key groups of stakeholders, along with objectives for communication, the message, and types of communication.

Employees

The goal of these early communications covers a range purposes: establishing a dialog, reducing uncertainty, building strategic ownership, identifying issues and concerns, addressing misperceptions, and uncovering roadblocks.

From my experience at both Nike and Coors, an effective approach with employees is to meet with groups of around 20 in an informal town hall setting with a Q&A format. The employees can be randomly selected, function leaders, local teams, etc. In an organization of scale it is also important to use a mix of broader communications vehicles as well such as blogs, all-employee presentations, or newsletters.

Franchisees, Owners, and Customers

The first 100 days represent a unique chance to revitalize relationships by building trust, sharing objectives, and showing a desire to listen. Key messages would be: 1) Starwood plans to continue its direction of building brands and being asset-light, 2) the new CEO's philosophy is all about partnership and finding win-win solutions, listening, and finding ways to improve profits together, and 3) the brand-led strategy is the key to better performance, but may require changes and investment.

Investment Community

The key objective in the first 100 days is to eliminate any concerns about whether Starwood will put aside its brand-led and asset-light strategy. The message would likely be that these strategies will continue, but that it is nonetheless important for the new CEO to review the strategy and the actions it implies. In the course of such a preliminary review, Starwood will communicate important actions based on this direction.

The Board

Especially in the beginning, it will be invaluable to take advantage of Board Members' insights and experience through an open dialog with the Board, in order to share emerging thoughts about strategies, the organization, costs, financial issues, and top team composition. This will also be an opportunity to manage and set appropriate expectations.

This could take a combination of weekly updates by email, 1x1 conversations, and formal presentations—whatever works best. The Board should expect the same candid open-mindedness, accessibility, and support from me as CEO, as I hope I have already demonstrated during the recruiting process. I also look forward to working directly with the Chairman. My own style is to be available virtually at all times by BlackBerry.

IV. INITIAL PERSPECTIVE ON THE ORGANIZATION

The structure should follow directly from the strategy and key business activities. No structure is perfect, nor is structure everything there is to organization, as processes and informal connections are valuable as well. The goal in the first 100 days is not to reorganize the company, but to develop a point of view on whether it is set up for success.

Barriers to be eliminated could include incentive systems that do not reward progress to strategic goals, unclear or overlapping responsibilities, lack of direction for a brand or region, too many or too few resources, absence of a process for launching innovation, or identifying that there is no formal way to incorporate guest or partner input.

The central structural issue for Starwood is balancing the matrix of functions, operations, regions, and brands. This was also true in my experience in designing the organizations for Disney Consumer Products (DCP) and at Nike. In both instances, the key was to identify the primary dimensions where the activities most directly drive value. In Nike, regions formed the primary dimension of the matrix, and for DCP it was line of business (Licensing, Publishing, Stores). The primary dimensions are where the P&Ls

lie and are managed. My preliminary view on Starwood is that brands are primary, supported by shared services at the global or regional levels.

Understanding the culture is also important. It can help to identify some symbolic actions to address weaknesses in the culture. For example, at Coors, alignment of the top team was a major issue, so within the first 100 days we presented as a team to the employees, initiated weekly meetings, and announced that all top team members' bonuses would be driven by the same criteria.

V. UNDERSTAND THE KEY FINANCIAL AND OPERATIONAL LEVERS

Nearly all of the key financial and operational issues will be touched in reviewing the strategy and the organization. Still, it is also important to take a top-down look at the business, particularly from a financial perspective. In today's deal-driven environment, the possibility of a private equity acquisition is real. From my outside vantage point, however, there is no other ownership structure for Starwood better than being public—as long as management does its job. So it is up to the new CEO, with support from the Board, to leverage the public ownership model to shareholders' best advantage. This means quickly probing company financial leverage, assets that should be sold, cost reductions, changes in strategy, along with other components of value creation.

The focus here will be to look at the company from the perspective of a private equity owner and to identify any major pre-emptive changes in capitalization, cost, foreign exchange risk, or operations.

SUMMARY

The five objectives represent a challenging but realistic set of expectations for the first 100 days. While this plan will no doubt change with the events and discoveries to come, the objectives are not likely to change much. The first 100 days are a great opportunity for a new CEO to set the stage for long-term success. The challenge is to balance the need to act with the need to learn. I am reminded of the wisdom in John Madden's line "be fast, but move slowly." As important as the first 100 days are, the real measure of success will be apparent in the first 18 months, as actions and their results are realized in the marketplace and in financial performance. I sincerely look forward to sharing that success with you.

5. USING EVIDENCE: LESSONS FROM THE CEO TRANSITION STUDY

When it comes to choosing the best person for a top leadership job, decision makers can be prone to make mistakes by relying on commonly held, but often misplaced, notions about what is the right thing to do. As we saw with Bill Perez at Nike and Wrigley, Tony Marx at the New York Public Library, Frits van Paasschen at Starwood Hotels, and other people leadership decisions detailed throughout the book, choosing a new leader (whether the CEO or another key position) is an extremely complicated and multifaceted business. Definitive rules, such as considering someone for a position *only* if the person has had experience doing the very same job before or assuming that candidates promoted from within are definitively *better* than those recruited from outside, can lead you astray. This chapter, which is built on the foundation of our CEO Transition Study but is applicable beyond the corner office, brings some empirical evidence to bear on the issue of who indeed is the right leader for a particular situation at a particular point in time. In so doing, we provide you with some tools to help you follow the second essential truth about leadership selection: once you have diagnosed the need, then you can get the very best person.

Let's start with the question of "insiders versus outsiders." Boards of directors and hiring managers often believe that recruiting a new executive from the outside is an admission of failure. This isn't surprising since they've been bombarded with a steady drumbeat of messages from management gurus, governance experts, and academics pushing the view that leaders promoted from within are superior to those recruited from outside because they supposedly outperform and are better for the organization. This opinion is so pervasive that it has become conventional wisdom. Organizational consulting firm RHR International, for example, wrote in its newsletter *Executive Insights* that "CEOs hired from outside are more likely than an internally developed leader to oversee poorer financial returns and fail at a higher rate." Management expert Ram Charan wrote in his February 2005 *Harvard Business Review* article, "Ending the CEO Succession Crisis," that one of "the trouble[s] with outsiders is that they import new management teams, causing a collapse of morale, continuity, and momentum." CEO coach Marshall Goldsmith opines, "Hiring an external successor brings great risk and sends the wrong message about [leadership] development [to an organization]. Effective internal succession produces the opposite, positive outcomes. Hiring an internal candidate shows that you have made the effort to develop internal talent."

These perspectives are compelling and deserve attention because of the prominence of the people advocating them, but the conclusions are simply not correct. Deeper analysis shows that overall there is no categorical performance difference between insider and outsider CEOs and that the right choice of a top leader is largely dependent on the situation. Why then, is this view so pervasive?

For one thing, there are a variety of ways to analyze the issue. The very act of judging CEO performance is challenging. Consulting firm Booz & Company (formerly Booz Allen & Hamilton) has been conducting a global study of CEO succession for a decade. They have data on more than three thousand CEO successions from around the world and use regionally adjusted average growth rates of total shareholder returns (including the reinvestment of dividends) to judge CEO track record. There are serious drawbacks to relying on total shareholder return as the sole measure of a CEO's performance. Yes, it is the most important report card issued by investors. But shareholder returns are highly dependent on the time period evaluated, so that measure can lead you to draw one conclusion at one point and to an altogether different one the next. Also, shareholder returns are only partially a result of things a CEO and an organization actually do—setting strategy, building a team, developing products, serving customers, generating revenue, controlling expenses, making investment decisions, executing M&A, and so on. A leadership team may do all of these things spectacularly well, but their results may not be reflected in the price of a company's stock. That may have more to do with what is happening in the broader economy, with investor sentiment, and with performance relative to expectations. Shareholder returns are thus an insufficient measuring stick of leadership performance, but should be part of a balanced scorecard that includes other quantitative criteria such as revenue and profit growth as well as qualitative criteria such as innovation, quality of the management team, and corporate reputation.

Another reason for the widespread belief that outsiders are at best a necessary evil is that the stories of leadership failure, often coupled with enormous severance payouts, receive much more media coverage and investor scrutiny than the success stories. Despite the fact that there are just as many successful outside CEOs as there are high-profile failures, who can forget, for example, the outcry surrounding the $210 million severance package paid to former Home Depot chief Bob Nardelli in early 2007?[4]

Given the heated point of view that many maintain about the problem of outsiders being brought in for key leadership positions and that the most influential study was based on a one-dimensional performance metric, we decided that the issue required empirical evidence to which we could apply our judgment and experience. So over a two-year period we conducted a CEO Transition Study covering the US, UK, German, French, and Dutch markets.[5] The first order of business was defining the analytical universe. For the US market, the S&P 500, comprising a broad array of companies in every industry sector, was chosen as the data set. For the other markets, the most commonly accepted company indices were also chosen. Specifically, in the United Kingdom, it was the *Financial Times*

4. Note that the vast majority of Nardelli's severance was from the contractual vesting of stock options that had been previously awarded since the time of his hiring in 2000; while Nardelli came under fire for his pay package as well as his directive management style, his CEO tenure also coincided with one of the most profitable periods in the history of the company.
5. Our US study, "Succeeding at Succession," was published in *Harvard Business Review,* November 2010.

"FTSE" index of the largest 150 companies; in France it was the CAC (40 companies); in the Netherlands, the AEX and the AMX (50 companies); and in Germany, the DAX and MDAX (80 companies). The five-year period from 2004 through 2008 was the time frame, long enough to perceive trends and diverse enough to cover both the robust economy of 2004 to 2007 and the financial crisis of 2008. For each transition—there were 463 in total—we performed a detailed case study.

We began our assessment by considering over twenty-five variables, including company condition, industry sector, where the CEO came from, whether the new leader was a first-time or experienced CEO, his or her functional background, and whether he or she had prior public company board experience. We then assessed the company's performance under the CEO based on three quantitative measures: shareholder returns relative to peer companies and the overall market; revenue growth; and profit growth. To gain a qualitative sense of the company's performance under the new CEO, we conducted interviews and examined public information. Specifically, we analyzed changes in the company's reputation, evidence of innovation, and the board's evaluation of CEO performance. We then ranked the CEOs into four performance quartiles: the CEOs in the top quartile were "outstanding," the middle two were "solid," and the bottom quartile were "poor." We were then able to analyze the data in countless ways, searching for trends, correlations, and causalities.

The findings were generally consistent across the five markets. Over this five-year time frame, CEO transitions averaged 11 percent a year overall (with a narrow range of 9 percent in the Netherlands to 12 percent in France and the United States). Insider CEOs were appointed just under two-thirds of the time (with a wider range of 56 percent in the United Kingdom to 74 percent in the Netherlands), and outsiders were brought in approximately a quarter of the time (with a range of 20 percent in the United States to 34 percent in the United Kingdom). The remaining cases (12 percent in all) were divided between CEOs who came off the board of directors, former employees brought back into the company as CEO, and executives recruited into the company as a number two and promoted within eighteen months to CEO (we call these cases "insider-outsiders").

The data provide definitive proof that the conventional wisdom stating that CEOs recruited from the outside underperform those promoted from within is simply not true. At the aggregate level, there is almost no difference in performance. Among the top quartile of CEO performers, there are roughly equal proportions of insiders and outsiders. So too is the case with the bottom quartile of CEO performers, essentially an equal proportion of insiders and outsiders.

The issue of whether insiders outperform outsiders—or vice versa—asks the wrong question. The right question turns out to be whether the business is healthy and growing or significantly challenged. The right person for the top leadership job is highly dependent on the company situation at the time. A healthy, growing company presents a fundamentally different leadership context than one facing a financial crisis. It will not surprise you to know that insiders are much more commonly promoted to CEO when a company is in healthy condition. Roughly three-quarters of all CEOs appointed in healthy companies were promoted from within, whereas only 17 percent were brought in from the outside (the remaining 10 percent were board members, former employees, or insider-outsiders).

Not surprisingly, outsiders are much more common when companies find themselves in a challenged situation or, worse, facing financial crisis. At challenged companies, those facing at least three consecutive quarters of underperforming their industry peer group, 39 percent of CEO appointments were outsiders, whereas 44 percent were promoted from within (the

CEO Origin at Healthy Companies
U.S. S&P 500, U.K. FTSE 150, French CAC 40, German DAX/MDAX 80, and Dutch AEX/AMX 50

Insiders at Healthy Companies:
U.S. 73% of S&P 500 Companies; U.K. 64% of FTSE 150; France 63% of CAC (40); Germany 73% of DAX/MDAX (80); and Netherlands 61% of AEX/AMX (50)

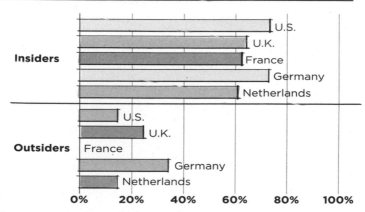

Source: Spencer Stuart CEO Transition Study

CEO Origin at Challenged Companies
U.S. S&P 500, U.K. FTSE 150, French CAC 40, German DAX/MDAX 80, and Dutch AEX/AMX 50

Insiders at Challenged Companies:
U.S. 27% of S&P 500 Companies; U.K. 36% of FTSE 150; France 38% of CAC (40); Germany 28% of DAX/MDAX (80); and Netherlands 39% of AEX/AMX (50)

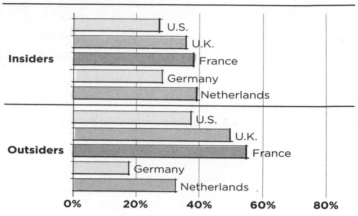

Source: Spencer Stuart CEO Transition Study

remaining 17 percent were either board members, former employees, or insider-outsiders).

When a company is healthy, the analysis shows that insiders outperform outsiders. The empirical data are rather overwhelming. In the United States, for example, insider appointments of healthy companies were *three times more likely* than outsiders to have achieved top-quartile performance. Outsiders fell into the lowest-performing quartile at more than double the rate.

Why is this the case?

For one thing, healthy companies tend to produce leadership talent in a virtuous circle of cause and effect. The stronger the company, the greater its magnetism for attracting raw talent in the first place and the more resources it is able to devote to management development. This in turn develops better managers who of course help the organization achieve better results, keeping the positive cycle rolling along. Over time, cream rises to the top of these organizations, producing strong and potentially viable succession candidates.

For another, healthy growing companies generally develop strong cultures that make it difficult for outsiders to fit in. At high-performing organizations their cultures generally exert a positive-meets-positive polar force that repels outsiders, especially at the top. Exhibit A is Nike and the case of Bill Perez. When a business or any organization is very successful, company leaders believe their way of doing things is right and resist outsiders who challenge them. *What do they know? We're the ones who are leading the market.*

The boards of healthy growing companies have fewer crises and have the necessary time to devote to the long and hard work of leadership succession. They are able to spend literally years on CEO succession, conducting annual deep-dive talent reviews, giving members of the senior management team opportunities to get to know directors in formal and less-formal settings, and using organizational moves to expand prospective internal candidates' experiences into new functional areas, different businesses, and international geographies. The board of Procter & Gamble, for example, started working on the succession of A. G. Lafley in his earliest days as CEO, leading to the promotions of Robert McDonald from president of the Global Fabric and Home Care business in 2001, to vice chairman and president of global operations in 2004, and then to chief operating officer in 2007. Before he was finally chosen to become president and CEO in 2009, he had been tested and assessed in each of his roles, he had presented business reviews and strategic plans to the board, and he had interacted with the investment community. There were other internal candidates who were put through similar steps and evaluated along the way. But the more exposure the board had to McDonald over this time frame, the more confidence they had that he was the very best leader to accelerate the strategies and sustain the culture that have made P&G the worldwide consumer-products market leader.

A company facing a liquidity crisis or a hostile acquisition does not have this luxury. It is not too surprising that most senior-level businesspeople have come to expect that when a company is in crisis and needs to make sweeping changes, one of those changes is to reach outside for new leadership. The granddaddy of external CEO recruitments, the bellwether of outside hires against which every case since has been measured, goes all the way back to 1993, when IBM brought in Louis V. Gerstner from RJR Nabisco to lead one of the world's most iconic companies. Before then it would have been inconceivable for IBM, one of the world's largest companies, to bring in a CEO from the outside. It was as if that play was not in the board of directors' playbook. But given how visibly successful Gerstner was in turning around—indeed saving—IBM, it became a plausible leadership option to go outside for a new CEO when a company was in trouble. For years afterward, directors would say, "We need *a Lou Gerstner* to come in and turn around our company." Today, few would bat an eyelash or question the wisdom when a troubled company goes outside for new leadership, such as was the case in recent years at AIG, AOL, A&P, Carrefour, Computer Associates, Ford Motor, Gap, and Nokia to name a few.

We've seen that outsiders are not only the exception when it comes to selecting leadership for healthy companies, but that as a group they significantly underperform insiders in this situation. And as detailed in the preceding, outsiders, not surprisingly, are much more common when a company is in trouble. Not only are they more common, however. When a company is in a significantly challenged or crisis condition, the data show overwhelmingly that outsiders outperform insiders. In fact, across all markets, outsiders achieved top-quartile performance at double the rate of insiders. Specifically in the US market, outsiders were three times as likely to achieve top-quartile performance. On the flip side, our international study showed that insiders were three times more likely to perform in the bottom performance quartile than outsiders.

Let's delve into the reasons why this is the case.

A company in crisis, with diminished standing among the investment community, customers, employees, or regulatory authorities or in desperate need of a turnaround or strategic redirection, will be more receptive to an outsider, especially a well-known person coming in as CEO to start a new chapter for the organization. It's often akin to the organization hitting the reset button, allowing long-held assumptions, power bases, and ways of doing business to be questioned. Outsiders brought in at challenged companies benefit from new eyes and fresh perspective and have few if any ties to the prior regime.

They are free of the baggage or blame associated with the company's current challenges and are able to ask questions that have long been considered off-limits. And since they do not feel obliged to support historically powerful internal constituencies, they have the opportunity more readily to make fundamental changes.

Insiders, by contrast, are often captive of the culture that got the company into the crisis in the first place. They also have friendships and relationships throughout the organization that have been developed over time, making it more difficult to implement the necessary change.

Perhaps no recent case illustrates what the appropriate outside leader can do to right a ship as well as Alan Mulally at Ford Motor Company. Having joined the world's second-largest automaker in 2006 from Boeing, where he was executive vice president and president and CEO of commercial airplanes, Mulally has done many of the things that are so difficult for an insider to do with a large organization that finds itself in a difficult predicament. He challenged long-held notions of the way things were done around Ford and cut some important ties with the past while preserving others. Specifically, when he started at the company, everybody told him to cut costs and then cut some more. But he believed that technical advancement and innovation were the keys to the company's long-term success, so he started questioning the management team about what a sustainable Ford would look like, how it was going to grow, and what it had to do to create value.

Mulally cut truck production in the face of rising gasoline prices and pared down the company's sprawling portfolio of businesses. He sold off the prestigious brands that comprised the luxury division, Jaguar, Aston Martin, and Volvo, as well as relinquishing twelve years of control of Mazda Motor through the sale of a 20 percent stake in the Japanese carmaker. Most significantly, Mulally led a redirection of billions of dollars of capital investment to shift Ford's production from pickups and SUVs to small cars. Logical as these moves seem after the fact with the evident shift in consumer demand, this was a fundamental reinvention of the way that the Big Three did business, long relying on sales of big, profitable SUVs and trucks. He challenged what had come to be assumed as a self-evident truth in the North American auto business, that you couldn't make money in small cars. But he repeatedly asked, "Why can't *we* make money on small cars? Do you think Toyota can't make money on small cars?"

Mulally's leadership has paid off handsomely for the company and its shareholders. Over his tenure as CEO, Ford was the only one of the Big Three that refused to take federal bailout money; plus it has seen its market value more than double and its corporate reputation soar.

For an outsider to succeed as CEO, even taking over a company in crisis, there are two absolute must-haves. The first is credibility. Credibility is derived from a track record of successful previous accomplishment combined with enough relevant experience that the appointment comes across as logical. When a new leader is announced, you can be sure that just about everyone inside the organization will rush to check him or her out on Google and ask those who might know the person what they think. The early feedback will set the tone for how the new leader is received. When there is a lack of credibility, a new leader is severely handicapped or worse.

In late 2008, the Association of Tennis Professionals (ATP Tour), the worldwide governing body of men's professional tennis was looking for a new CEO. The search committee wanted to identify prospective candidates along two axes, geography and industry. Professional tennis was shifting from an American to a European orientation as the Pete Sampras and Andre Agassi era gave way to the dominance of Roger Federer from Switzerland and Rafael Nadal from Spain. The new CEO would have to have professional and life experience in Europe as well as in the United States and Asia ideally. From an industry perspective, the majority of the search committee wanted candidates who were former professional tennis players who had gone on to distinguished private- or public-sector careers, executives in the business of tennis or sports more broadly, and possibly strong general management leaders who had a demonstrated commitment to and passion for tennis. When one of the search committee members expressed an initial preference for a strong general manager from a global corporation versus a candidate with a connection to tennis, it was pointed out that the success rate of industry outsiders recruited into top leadership roles in the sports industry was less than 20 percent. Less than *one in five* nonsports executives had transitioned successfully into the business of sports. Whether it was the string of CEOs of the US Olympic Committee having come from corporate positions (such as Lloyd Ward of Maytag, Norman Blake of Promus Hotels and USF&G, and Stephanie Streeter of Banta Corporation), or the short-lived tenure of Gregory Murphy, the former Kraft General Foods executive hired to run Major League Baseball Enterprises, the sports industry has been littered with outsiders who ultimately did not take hold.

Knowledge is an important dimension of credibility. As Justin Gimelstob, the former number 63 ranked tennis player in the world, one of the seven elected members of the ATP board, and a leader of the search committee, succinctly put it, "All a new CEO would have to say to a tour player is 'Good *game*' rather than 'Good *match*' and he would be dead on the spot." It did not take too much discussion for the committee to agree that the focus of their search would be leaders with a genuine connection to tennis and the business of sports.

In the end, the committee recruited Adam Helfant, the former Nike global sports marketing corporate vice president. Helfant, an MIT and Harvard Law graduate, brought to the ATP a career of global sports, business, and legal experience, including twelve years at Nike, three years with the National Hockey League (NHL) as an attorney, and four years as an associate at an international law firm. At Nike, where he was responsible for the company's relationships and contracts with athletes, sports clubs, professional teams, universities, and sports governing bodies throughout the world, he led negotiations for over $1 billion worth of sponsorship deals.

In his two years leading the ATP, Helfant won plaudits for his thorough, low-key approach to improving the relationships between players and tournament organizers, working to rationalize the debilitating year-round professional tour calendar, further globalizing the sport through marketing and media programs, and securing a new tourwide sponsor to replace Mercedes-Benz.

The second must-have for outsiders to become effective is a set of personal traits, such as being an effective listener and a fast learner and possessing self-confidence without hubris. One cannot make up for personality or character shortcomings. But if an executive has the intellect, energy, passion, and capacity to perform well, and the humility to recognize what she still needs to learn, she then has the foundational ingredients for success. For an outside leader to be successful, she needs to have the confidence and an ego that is in check to surround herself with managers who can complement her skills. And perhaps most important, as an outsider she needs to earn the trust and confidence of those with tenure in the company to share their company and industry knowledge.

The key message of this chapter so far is that in order to choose the best leader for a top job, you need to diagnose the situation carefully and match the right leader to that situation. If a company is healthy and growing, there should be a strong preference for promoting from within because insiders dramatically outperform outsiders in these cases. If a company is in a significantly challenged state or crisis, however, then outsiders have generally been proven to be the better leadership solution.

Before setting this guidance into concrete, bear in mind that there are two important exceptions. The first is something we call the "pendulum effect," that is, a board swinging from one extreme to another, often without even considering an alternative. Specifically, when there is a high-profile outsider CEO who fails visibly, even for a company in crisis, the board has a strong inclination to default to an insider. The thinking is, *Well, going outside sure didn't work last time, so this time we are going to stay inside.* As it happens, this is often the right decision. After a failed externally hired leader, the organization rallies around the insider successor and works overtime to compensate for any experience gaps.

Such was the case when Mark Parker was chosen to succeed Bill Perez at Nike and when Frank Blake was promoted from the inside to replace Bob Nardelli at Home Depot in January 2007. Blake had served as executive vice president of business development and corporate operations from March 2002 to January 2007, where he was responsible for the Home Depot's real estate, store construction, credit services, strategic business development, growth initiatives, international, call centers, and services businesses.

Perhaps the best example of the pendulum effect was at Xerox Corporation when Anne Mulcahy, a longtime, beloved insider, became in the words of *Fortune* magazine, "The Accidental CEO." Rick Thoman, one of the most well-respected senior executives at IBM—he was chief financial officer and had run the company's PC business—had been recruited to Xerox as president in 1997 and was appointed CEO in 1999. But despite his blue-chip credentials, under his direction Xerox went on the skids. In 2000, amid a shutdown of the credit markets, Xerox had $17 billion in debt and only $154 million in cash on the balance sheet, its market value had fallen 90 percent, and it was shedding market share precipitously (Japanese competitors were eating Xerox's lunch in their core copier business and HP was dominating in printers). It was about to begin seven straight quarters of losing money, and bankruptcy was looming. Even worse, the company had been accused of perpetrating a major accounting scandal. The SEC charged that it had defrauded investors by improperly accelerating revenues, overstating earnings by using fictitious reserves, and disguising loans as asset sales.[6]

When Thoman was ousted in May 2000 after only thirteen months on the job, Mulcahy agreed to become president and CEO-in-waiting, working for former CEO Paul Allaire, who had stepped back into the CEO role. Although she became CEO in August 2001 and chairman in January 2002, Mulcahy was quick to admit that her career path was not designed to be that of a Fortune 500 CEO. She had spent sixteen of her twenty-four years at Xerox in sales before becoming the head of human resources and chief of staff to the CEO. She had less than a year and a half in a P&L job, having created a fledgling desktop business to go against HP printers. She did not have an MBA, but rather a journalism degree from Marymount College, and had never sat on a board of directors. "I was never groomed to be CEO of Xerox," says Mulcahy. "It was a total surprise to everyone, including myself."

But she had many of the qualities that make for a highly effective CEO—and then some. Mulcahy was disciplined, nonpolitical, hardworking, compassionate yet tough, and completely dedicated to Xerox (her husband and brother had both also had long and successful careers at the company). Her

---

6. In June 2003, former CEOs Paul Allaire and Rick Thoman and four other former Xerox executives settled individual SEC charges neither admitting nor denying wrongdoing; they agreed to pay more than $22 million in penalties and fines.

leadership by example and obvious dedication to lead the company out of its morass gave her enormous credibility, which galvanized the organization. Employees did not want to let her down. She implored them to save dollars at every opportunity and spend money as if it was their own. The company and culture responded. In some regions, the field sales organization eliminated expensive compensation incentives and instead rewarded top producers with ceremonial car washes performed by colleagues. Mulcahy said that people were even holding prayer groups and saying the rosary for her. It is hard to imagine an outside CEO generating that kind of emotional support.

Their support was rewarded. Over her leadership tenure, Mulcahy not only helped Xerox stave off bankruptcy but is credited with turning the company around. The company then went on to engineer the first Fortune 500 woman-to-woman CEO handoff. On July 1, 2009, Mulcahy was succeeded by another insider CEO, longtime colleague Ursula Burns (who also became the first ever female African American CEO in the Fortune 500).

The second exception to the insiders-to-healthy-companies, outsiders-to-challenged-companies guidance is actually a hybrid approach. In a minority of cases, 5 percent across the five markets in our CEO Transition Study, CEOs have come from the board of directors. This is a powerful exception and something to keep in mind because CEOs appointed from the board have been the highest-performing group of leaders of any category—stronger than insiders, outsiders, former executives, or insider-outsiders. In challenged companies, in particular, they have dramatically outperformed with double the rate of top-quartile versus bottom-quartile CEO performance. Board members turned CEO are a bridge between outsider and insider. They have more company knowledge than a pure outsider, but they don't have the constraints of an insider when it comes to making unpopular decisions and leading necessary but painful change.

Michael Roth became CEO of the Interpublic Group (IPG) of Companies on January 19, 2005. He had been elected to the board in 2002 and after serving as chairman of the audit committee, he agreed to become chairman of the board in July 2004 to contend with the company's mounting accounting scandal and financial crisis. Following a special meeting of the board in early 2005, to which he was not invited, Roth was asked to step into the CEO role and he agreed. Drawing on his three years of experience participating in board discussions, Roth benefited from proprietary insight into the company's competitive positioning, the strengths and weaknesses of its management team, and liquidity and balance sheet considerations. As a result, he had a substantial head start in understanding and prioritizing the company's key issues. He had also built strong relationships with his fellow directors and had a feel for the group dynamics of the board, which enabled him more confidently to develop his action plan and know which directors could provide what kind of support.

There are two ways a board member can become the CEO, "pull" and "push." Pull is when the board comes to the conclusion that one of its own is in fact the best person to assume the top job and asks—or more typically pleads with—a director to consider taking on the ultimate responsibility. Such was the case with Roth and IPG. He told us he was surprised when the board even wanted to discuss it. "They informed me that they were going to have a special board meeting. I told them, 'Hey, I'm the chairman. You can't have a board meeting without me!' They said they would call me in after some discussion." When he was told that the board unanimously voted that he should become CEO, he accepted on the condition that they not require him to sign a long-term contract. He said that he would serve at the pleasure of the board until they wanted him to and no longer. "As chairman I felt like I was in a small plane that was going down, but I was stuck in the backseat. I figured that I might as well accept the responsibility, move into the pilot seat, and try and bring the plane out of its nose dive," he analogized.

The board wanted Roth so badly because he was known as a fiscal hawk on the board and a turnaround CEO. In his career before IPG, he had spent fourteen years at the MONY Group, taking a life assurance company on the verge of bankruptcy and turning it into a successful diversified financial services business before its acquisition by French insurance giant AXA Group for $1.5 billion in 2003. Interpublic, whose advertising agencies include McCann WorldGroup, Lowe Worldwide, and Draftfcb, had struggled since the late 1990s when it had problems integrating and running the companies it bought in an acquisition spree. An accounting scandal broke in 2002, and the company was the subject of a US Securities and Exchange Commission probe just as it was under severe pressure to pare debt and turn around its loss-making operations. Clients were fleeing as well. After losing the prestigious

Coca-Cola account, the Universal McCann media division lost the important Nestlé business as well.

Roth embarked on a restructuring program by integrating IPG's Draft and FCB units and aligning the sprawling media services brands into a coherent organizational structure. From there he was able to take out costs and facilitate the diverse and often competing agency networks to work more effectively together to serve clients in a more holistic and strategic way. Roth brought in new top management talent to key functional roles, and with the insight gleaned from his time on the board he was able to redeploy certain IPG executives into roles that took better advantage of their client and creative strengths. While restructuring and rationalizing, Roth also invested in the exploding digital and social media sector, which was becoming more central to its clients around the world. In 2007, IPG formed a partnership with web services company Spongecell, acquired Reprise Media, a provider of search engine marketing solutions, and entered into a strategic partnership with BzzAgent, a word-of-mouth media network, to facilitate the development of grassroots campaigns for its agencies' clients. Roth also made an early investment in Facebook to gain strategic insight into the social media space (IPG's investment of less than $5 million had a market value of approximately $200 million at the most recent valuation). In 2008, the company focused on expanding its reach into growth markets, completing transactions in the Middle East and North Africa regions, and continued to acquire a number of independent interactive agencies to create sustainable online businesses. It also finally settled the longtime accounting probe by the SEC, agreeing to pay $12 million in penalties.

As a result of these efforts, IPG was able to return to profitability with industry-matching-or-beating organic revenue growth, a cleaner balance sheet, and a stronger corporate reputation. Clients responded favorably. In January 2008, for example, IPG's Initiative unit was selected as the media agency of record by Hyundai Motors America and Kia Motors America. The company also experienced significant industry recognition, being named "Comeback Agency of the Year" by *Advertising Age* in 2008. Roth has proven to be just the right leader for the challenging Interpublic situation. He was able to bring the dispassion of an outsider to his cost reduction, restructuring, and regulatory settlement efforts while making the management, organizational, and M&A moves of a savvy insider.

But it doesn't always work out so smoothly when the situation is a "push." An uncomfortable dynamic can be unleashed when a board member, usually retired, decides that he would like the job himself in the wake of a departing CEO. The thought process goes something like this: *I've been a successful executive prior to joining this board and I know this business as well as anyone around the table. And I miss the action. . . . Yes, I think I'll go for it.* The board member then has to figure out who to talk to and what to say. That's when it gets really tricky.

One scenario went like this. The CEO of an S&P 500 company was removed for performance reasons. The nonexecutive chairman agreed to become interim CEO, and he was the natural director to chair the board's search committee. But having him chair the committee was the right decision if—and only if—he was certain that he did not want to be a candidate for the CEO job himself. There are many cases where interim CEOs decide that they enjoy being in—or often *back in*—the saddle. They forget how much they enjoyed operating versus governing. They remember how good it feels to implement rather than advise and be the ultimate arbiter of key issues. So they decide to go for it. While the chairman promised that he had no interest in or intention of wanting the full-time job, it would have been prudent to have one of the independent directors chair the committee. About a month later, a monster started to rear its ugly head. The chairman/interim CEO felt the adrenaline rush of reorganizing the management team, visiting major customers, and leading the investor calls. The industry analysts started writing positive reviews of his decisiveness and smart moves. He told the head of the search committee that he was utterly surprised that he thought he now actually wanted the CEO post. "I've never felt so energized," he beamed. There was just one problem. As effective as he was as the chairman, and he was a very good chairman, it was not at all clear how he would perform as permanent CEO. This put the committee into a real pickle.

The board had appointed the previous CEO two years earlier without a rigorous search process and had suffered severe criticism and several shareholder lawsuits when they ousted him. So they had made a very big deal about how they were going to conduct a comprehensive global search, considering internal and external candidates until they found the very best leader for the company. The committee could not come back to the full board and say, *Just kidding! Now that the chairman has unilaterally decided he wants the job, we're going to give it to him.* The chairman put himself at risk as well. In throwing his hat into the ring, what would happen if he didn't get the job? How would he be able to go back to being an effective chairman if he failed to win the support of the board?

In private, one of the influential members of the search committee asked the chairman to hold off and not officially declare his interest. An analysis was done of the chairman's earlier CEO performance, the same rigorous assessment being given all other candidates. References were checked with board members and executives from his former company. What became quite clear was that his track record did not stack up when compared to the external candidates', all of whom had successful public company or general management operating experience at a $5-billion-plus scale. The chairman simply didn't have the credentials. His company had been smaller, and it was not particularly successful under his watch. It had largely domestic operations compared to the global reach of this company. This assessment was shared with him in a private meeting, and he was told that he would probably not get the CEO job if he went for it given the strength of the external slate. Moreover, it was explained that if he did throw his hat in the ring and was not chosen, he would have to seriously consider resigning from the board. On the positive side, it had been proven that his skill set had lent itself much more to his being chairman than CEO anyway. Perhaps the clinching argument was being reminded that he had promised his wife that he wouldn't become CEO again. He withdrew his interest from the job and went on to help recruit a CEO who to this day is performing at a superb level, and he is continuing to enjoy his role as nonexecutive chairman.

Another instance did not have this kind of storybook ending. A different company with a strong-willed, directive chairman was searching for a CEO. One month into the process the chairman decided that he wanted the corner office full-time. He presented the idea to his board, which was weak and tended to submit to the opinion of the chairman. There was not much discussion—there rarely was at his board meetings—and without much enthusiasm, the board agreed to ratify the chairman's own decision. The search process was aborted, and the chairman was announced as the permanent CEO. Even though the stock popped on the news—the analysts had been calling for a new CEO to be tough to revitalize the company—the reaction inside the company was not at all positive. Many in the organization felt as if the chairman had hijacked the company, and they were not far off the mark. As the new CEO, he didn't solicit or engender broad support from the employees, the executive team, even the board. No growth strategies were implemented, and an exodus of top management talent ensued. After the immediate analyst enthusiasm, the company soon lost the confidence of the investment community and the company has meandered to this day with subpar performance.

6. AVOIDING THE "RED HERRINGS" OF AGE, EXPERIENCE, AND ETHNICITY[7]

You have diagnosed the situation, now recognizing that choosing the best leader for a top position is not just about finding a "great" individual, but rather about solving an intricate and dynamic jigsaw puzzle. You have carefully considered empirical evidence from hundreds of top leadership successions across five of the world's largest markets that show the circumstances under which different leadership appointments have worked out best, and you are ready to develop a framework for choosing the person who is the very best fit for this specific job. You are almost ready. But before applying these first two essential truths of leadership selection, you need to recognize several factors that are often considered, but that turn out to be unimportant at best, misdirected at worst, in predicting the performance of a senior executive. This chapter identifies these "red herring" considerations so that you can ignore them—or at least put them into the right perspective—in choosing the right person for your organization. The potential red herrings as they pertain to the second essential truth,

---

7. *Red herring* (n.) is an idiomatic expression referring to the rhetorical tactic of diverting attention from the real problem or matter at hand; a misleading clue. See *The American Heritage Dictionary of the English Language*, Fourth Edition.

selecting the right person, have to do with age, experience, and ethnicity.

AGE

At senior management levels, one factor that has no correlation with—much less causality to—success is age. If you are recruiting in the United States, you probably know that using age as a decision criterion not only is politically incorrect but is a form of discrimination and therefore illegal.[8] Equally important, from a performance perspective, there is no case for setting age as a precondition when deciding upon the next senior executive hire or CEO. This is not to say that hiring managers and boards don't *think about* age in their leadership decisions. They do so all the time. In fact, age is often the very first thing that they talk about—even though they know they shouldn't—when describing the target profile: *We're looking for a CEO fifty to fifty-five years old who* . . . Don't be one of those people. Have the confidence to know that age is a red herring. Of course, for any senior leadership position, it is obviously essential that a younger candidate have sufficient management experience, just as it is crucial for a more seasoned executive to have the necessary energy and drive to deliver successful performance.

The CEO Transition Study yields evidence to support the

---

8. The Equal Opportunity Act (1995) and subsequent amendments make it unlawful for an employer or potential employer to discriminate against a person on the grounds of status or private life, including such factors as gender, physical or mental impairment, race, religion, industrial activity (e.g., belonging to a union), sexual orientation, physical characteristics (e.g., weight, height), marital status, *or* age.

fact that even beyond the law, age should be ignored when a candidate is qualified relative to those key selection criteria that have been thoughtfully developed and tailored to the situation at hand. Among the three hundred CEO transitions in S&P 500 companies over the 2004 to 2008 time frame, over half of the appointments were individuals in their fifties, 30 percent were in their forties, and 10 percent were in their sixties. There were even four new CEOs under the age of forty at the time of their appointment. But as illustrated in the chart,

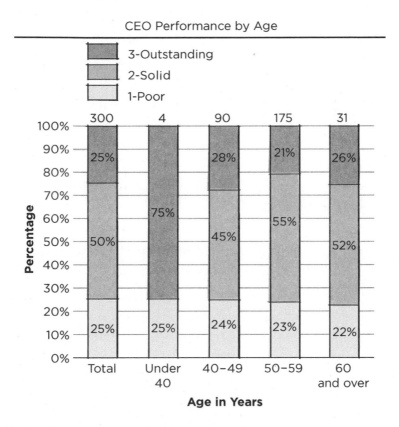

CEO Performance by Age

no particular group (other than the tiny number of cases of the under-40 CEOs) fared dramatically better or worse in terms of top-, or bottom-, quartile performance.

During the spring of 2007, Fox and NBC Universal were looking for the most talented digital media leader to take the helm of the new company that would have exclusive online video rights for their content. Their assumption going into the search was that the most visible and experienced Internet and digital media executives would be the right ones to take the helm of this business that was intended to confront the growing power and competitive threat of YouTube. Peter Chernin, then president and chief operating officer of Fox's parent company, News Corporation, and Jeff Zucker, then chairman and CEO of NBC Universal (himself a former child prodigy in the television business), were coleading this search and met six executives who were in their forties and early fifties. But when thirty-five-year-old Jason Kilar came into the picture, after initial skepticism due to his youth, it became clear to Chernin and Zucker that the then unknown executive was the right person to build the business that would become Hulu.

After graduating from the University of North Carolina– Chapel Hill in 1993, Kilar joined the Walt Disney Company. He worked for Disney Design & Development in the division's vacation club business. After two years with Disney, Kilar enrolled in Harvard Business School, where he focused his studies on the media and entertainment business. Having been introduced to an ambitious young entrepreneur in a class called "Managing in the Marketplace," Kilar decided to ignore the conventional MBA career route of investment banking or consulting and even demurred from joining a major media company after graduation. Instead he followed an inspiring visionary to Seattle. The entrepreneur was none other than Jeff Bezos, and the company was a fledgling online book retailer called Amazon.com.

Kilar spent the next nine years at Amazon.com becoming one of the company's most important business builders. He began in the marketing department and was quickly dispatched by Bezos to enter new product areas to push beyond the core business of bookselling. Kilar determined that the most logical new segment, given that it shared many characteristics of bookselling, was video, both DVD and VHS. So he developed a business plan and colaunched Amazon.com's foray into that business and added other media products such as music. Over time, including the book business, Kilar was ultimately responsible for $2 billion in revenue. In 2002, Bezos asked Kilar to lead the Worldwide Application Software business, where he took on responsibility for the entire customer experience on Amazon.com. This was formative for Kilar in that it instilled an ethic and mind-set that has been one of the most important reasons for the company's stunning success over the years: that everything the company does should be evaluated through the lens of the consumer experience. Does a change or an enhancement make the website easier to use and more intuitive? Does a new business or feature fit seamlessly into the whole in a coherent way? From this way of thinking, Kilar was involved with teams that developed such features as One-Click ordering and offerings such as the Amazon merchant business, which dramatically increased the scope of products offered but did so within the framework and customer experience of Amazon.com.

After four years in this job, Kilar decided it was time to leave Amazon and focus his energies on the intersection of technology and media. He left the company on excellent terms and embarked on an ambitious yearlong trip around the world with his wife and young children. Soon after his return, he was working on an entrepreneurial venture developing a media content platform.

Here was the thought process that led Hulu to Kilar. At a meeting with Chernin and Zucker and their respective Fox and NBC project teams there was a heated discussion about why the new business, which had the project name "NewSite," would be successful. Most of the project team was arguing that because of the deep library of television shows and movies, consumers would flock to the site. Others were saying the differentiator would be the promotional power of the major media companies and their broadcast networks. But a small and insightful minority had a different view. They said that in the world of the web, where all television shows and movies would sooner or later find their way online, a deep library would not be sufficient. And as powerful as the broadcast networks were, you just had to look at the scale and power of Google, Facebook, and other relatively new players on the web to see that all the "old media" promotional power would amount to little. The only way to win would be to create the best site with the most compelling and intuitive user experience. That coupled with the other assets of the venture would be the best formula to win.

That insight became the guiding light of the search strategy for the leader of this new venture. Who provided consumers the best experience? Amazon.com. Who, other than Jeff Bezos, was the person most responsible for successfully creating that consumer experience? When various current and former Amazon executives were asked, the arrows pointed to Kilar. So he was tracked down and convinced that the opportunity to work with Fox, NBC, and potentially many other world-class partners would be much more compelling than continuing with his own venture. After several meetings he agreed, and in the summer of 2007, Kilar took the helm of the clunky-sounding joint venture "NewSite." Today Hulu garners over 900 million video streams per month and generates over $250 million in revenue. Kilar has accomplished all of this before the age of forty.

But success can come at any age. Consider the case of sixty-one-year-old Brian Duperreault, who took over Marsh & McLennan Companies after predecessor CEO Michael G. Cherkasky carried out a cleanup in the wake of lawsuits and investigations by the New York attorney general. The company's board appointed Duperreault, a highly experienced insurance executive, in an effort to improve the company's dismal finances and performance in 2004. Beginning his career as an actuary at AIG, Duperreault quickly rose through the ranks of the company as chief casualty officer, senior officer in Japan and Korea, and president of AIU Insurance, among other positions. In 1994, Duperreault took on the leadership of another insurance company, ACE Ltd., as chairman, president, and chief executive officer, where he served successfully for ten years before coming in to lead the turnaround of troubled Marsh & McLennan.

Under Duperreault's aggressive restructuring, the company saw an enormous increase in profits. He made many management changes, replacing more than four direct reports within his first year, simplified the organization structure to provide clearer accountabilities, created a new cross-company chief information officer role, and replaced the CEO of the company's risk consulting and technology unit. He also implemented a policy to cap Marsh's liability to $10 million per client in an effort to guard against future catastrophes. Overall, Duperreault restored the company's image and took Marsh & McLennan from being a clear market underperformer to an industry leader.

EXPERIENCE

As you well know, credibility is derived from a track record of successful previous accomplishment combined with experience sufficiently relevant that an appointment to a key leadership job is seen as logical—that is, all stakeholders see it as successfully putting in place the last piece of a complex jigsaw puzzle. However, within the broad parameters of what constitutes experience there are different interpretations of what constitutes "sufficiently relevant." When it comes to recruiting a top leader from outside an organization, one common issue that is debated is whether the finalist candidate is required to have done the job before—*We want someone who has "been there done that."* But is it correct automatically to assume that the new leader should have in fact "been there and done that"? In the case of public company CEO searches, how important is it for a candidate to have successful prior public company CEO experience? What about functional leaders such as chief financial officers? Does the not-for-profit sector differ from the business world as it relates to bringing in a new leader from the outside?

When it comes to choosing leaders for public companies, the data from the CEO Transition Study suggest that first-time CEOs recruited externally actually perform in line with CEOs with prior public company experience. The issue of experience is not of course unique to the case of choosing a CEO, but relates to other functions across the organization. When is it the right decision, for instance, to promote a marketing director into the chief marketing officer role, or a vice president of human resources into the chief HR officer position, or the senior IT manager into the chief information officer role? The same question applies in all functions and divisions in a company. To illustrate, let's delve into the finance function and consider when promoting a treasurer, corporate controller, or divisional financial executive is the right choice to become a company's chief financial officer and when it is necessary to bring in a CFO from the outside who has "been there done that." And when is an outsider who is a step-up candidate the right choice?

In the United States, each year between 2005 and 2010, there has been an average of seventy-six chief financial officer transitions among Fortune 500 companies, 15 percent a year. CFO turnover has ranged between 12 percent and 20 percent

annually over these five years. Sixty percent of these CFO appointments have been promoted from within, and 40 percent
have been recruited from the outside.[9] When a CFO leaves a
company either due to retirement, promotion into another role,
or being recruited away, or when a change needs to be made
for performance reasons, many chief executives and boards
of directors (typically the chair of the audit committee of the
board is directly involved in CFO selections) make assumptions similar to those of CEO search committees, that they
want a "proven public company CFO." However, it turns out
that only approximately 20 percent of Fortune 500 companies
appoint CFOs with public company CFO experience (an additional 5 percent have prior CFO experience in private companies or not-for-profit institutions). The principal reason why
this number is so low is that sitting public company CFOs are
reticent to move laterally. Those who are performing well in
their current role recognize that their effectiveness is a function not only of their own skills but also their relationships with
the CFO, the board and audit committee, other financial and
business executives across the organization, and often with key
investors and analysts. To move to another company means to
rebuild these internal and external networks, which involves
enormous work and not insignificant risk. The opportunity, in
terms of career and financial upside, has to be well worth the
effort and risk.

Another reason why the vast majority of new CFOs do not
come from sitting CFO ranks is that the CFO skill set continues

9. Source: Spencer Stuart CFO Transition Study; Financial Officers Practice
analysis.

to evolve, and the candidate pool would be too restrictive to focus only on those who had been in the roles in the past. For example, in the 1980s deal-driven corporate finance world, bankers were in vogue as CFOs to help propel companies in that decade's rapidly growing economy. In the post-Enron, Sarbanes-Oxley era, accounting and control-oriented backgrounds were in favor. More recently, capital markets/rating agency/regulator-savvy executives have been in greatest demand to help companies restore the health of their balance sheets and position themselves most favorably from a regulatory perspective.[10]

There are scenarios, of course, when public-company-experienced CFOs move into that same role at another organization. The most common reason is an increase in the scale and challenge of the job. Along with larger size is increased compensation as well, approximately 20 percent for laterally recruited CFOs. One person who made this determination not once but twice was Chris Liddell, the former vice chairman and chief financial officer of General Motors, who started with the company in January 2010. Liddell, a New Zealand native, had been CFO at Microsoft from 2005 to 2009, where he had responsibility for the software giant's financial operations, treasury, accounting, investor relations, and corporate strategy. He joined Microsoft from International Paper, where he was also finance chief. Liddell was the automaker's highest-profile hire

---

10. The greatest spike in CFO turnover, in 2007 when 20 percent of Fortune 500 companies appointed new CFOs, was driven by the need to drive the implementation of Sarbanes-Oxley requirements, not unlike the record-setting turnover in board audit committee chairs.

after its July 2009 bankruptcy, recruited by then chairman and CEO Ed Whitacre. "About half of the people I talked to about moving to GM thought I was crazy," he told us at the time. "It was risky from a career perspective to move to Detroit and join what many saw as a failing company that had taken on $50 billion in U.S. government bailout money. But to come into one of the world's most important and largest companies, which had gone through bankruptcy, and play a key role in one of the most significant turnarounds in business history; it doesn't get more exciting than that." He took on the challenge of restructuring operations, rebuilding the finance organization, and, most important, leading the largest initial public offering in US history. Liddell personally managed the $23 billion IPO across three continents, working with thirty-five underwriting banks. After nine months of in-depth planning; carefully setting roles between the company and its largest shareholder, the US government; developing the investor presentation; conducting ninety road show investor meetings around the world; working with rating agencies and commercial banks for a companion $5 billion debt offering; and in particular meeting with equity investors, including sovereign wealth funds and retail and major institutional investors, the offering was seven times oversubscribed. Liddell said that "The point of all these meetings was not only about securing immediate investor interest, but making a large number of interrelated market leaders and opinion makers believe in GM again." General Motors and its IPO was one of the major business success stories of 2010. Liddell's appointment as CFO was a case when it would have been unimaginable for a non-public-company-experienced CFO or an internal candidate to come into the role. His proven experience was essential for earning the credibility of the extensive GM organization, the newly structured board of directors (established when the company exited bankruptcy), the world's most prestigious investment bankers, and a skeptical business media. That being said, Liddell's lateral move to GM carried with it a limited timeline. Whereas his financial expertise and experience made him the right man for GM's unique needs pre-IPO, after fourteen months on the job, Liddell announced his resignation effective April 1, 2011, having concluded that the work he set out to do was successfully completed and deciding that he wanted to pursue a CEO position or other senior operating role.

By contrast, there are numerous examples of financial professionals who stepped up into the CFO role. One case that points out a common decision trade-off—scope versus scale—that has performed extremely well was when the fast-growing public Internet services company Akamai Technologies recruited J. D. Sherman as CFO in 2005. Sherman had been vice president, finance, of the Systems and Technology Group at IBM, which included servers, storage products, and semiconductors. The calculus of Paul Sagan, Akamai's CEO, and the board was that Sherman's experience at a division much larger in scale relative to the company—Akamai was under $1 billion in revenues and IBM Systems and Technology Group was $25 billion—coupled with his technology industry experience and financial expertise was sufficient to ensure credibility with the company's key constituents. At IBM, Sherman had been responsible for business planning, product pricing, operations, and financial controls for what was the largest systems company in the world with forty-five thousand employees and a $5 billion expense budget. These past professional responsibilities accompanied by his operational skills, sharp intellect, and leadership attributes were more than sufficient to give Akamai the confidence that Sherman could step up to the full scope of the public company CFO role.

Another important factor when it comes to recruiting a sitting CFO versus having to bring in a step-up candidate is location. Companies are often forced to look at a broader slate of candidates because the sitting public company CFO population with relevant industry experience is not willing to move to the location of the hiring company. This is not unique to the CFO role, of course; it's true across all the functions and at most levels of the company. The decision then comes down to deciding whether to hire an experienced CFO without industry experience or find a strong number two who knows the sector. Global online travel company Orbitz chose the former path, going outside the industry when it recruited fifty-three-year-old Russell Hammer as its new CFO in January 2011. The company determined that because Barney Harford, their talented thirty-eight-year-old chief executive, was relatively inexperienced in public company operations (prior to his appointment as CEO in January 2009 Harford had been in divisional roles at rival Expedia), it was more important for their new CFO to have public company know-how than travel or Internet industry experience. Hammer joined Orbitz from public company Crocs Inc., the maker of lightweight casual footwear, after a twenty-eight-year career at Motorola. When it comes to financial officers and other functional leaders, the key principle of leadership selection remains that the right choice is about finding not just a great executive but one who fits into the unique company puzzle at a specific time. The added dimension in solving a CFO or other C-suite puzzle is that personnel need to complement the experience and personality of a CEO.

Educational institutions and other not-for-profit organizations often make assumptions similar to those of the corporate world. Without question, when it comes to choosing their top leaders, the essential requirement that universities, colleges, cultural institutions, foundations, and nongovernmental organizations (NGOs) establish is for the new leader to have credibility with the people that he or she will oversee. For academic institutions this usually means a proven track record as a scholar and an educator. But the reality is that many fine scholars and educators who have made significant contributions to their respective fields have little interest in or aptitude for institutional leadership. Thus, if academic stature is the first criterion, the second is leadership ability. And that criterion is often articulated as "proven leadership," which in turn is distilled down to one question—Has a candidate successfully done the same job before? It is tempting, of course, to think that a person who has been successful in the role before is more likely to do it well a second time around. In university presidential search committees, for example, which are typically composed of members of the board of trustees, faculty, and the administration, it is often taken as a given that a sitting college or university president would be the ideal target profile.

However, as it turns out, this particular assumption is not necessarily well founded.

The highest-performing segment of presidents at the most
prestigious colleges and universities in the United States[11]
over the past two decades was actually first-time presidents.
Somewhat surprisingly, among the thirty appointments that
were made between 1990 and 2006 at these top universities,
a disproportionately large number of first-timers performed
in the top quartile of all university presidents.[12] A successful
prior career as a productive scholar and member of the faculty,
combined with some level of administrative experience and
the desired personal attributes, has often proved to be the best
profile.

For example, Jim Yong Kim, MD, PhD, the president of
Dartmouth College elected in March 2009, was previously
chair of the Department of Global Health and Social Medicine
at Harvard Medical School. An accomplished educator and
physician, over the nearly three decades since he graduated
from Brown University in 1982, Dr. Kim was known as a mo-
tivational teacher to students, trusted colleague to faculty, and
dedicated practitioner to fellow health professionals. In the
area of global health, as a former senior official at the World
Health Organization and cofounder of Partners in Health, a

---

11. Top 30 from *U.S. News & World Report* Ranking: Harvard, Princeton, Yale,
Caltech, MIT, Stanford, Penn, Columbia, U. Chicago, Duke, Dartmouth,
Northwestern, Washington U., Johns Hopkins, Cornell, Brown, Emory, Rice,
Vanderbilt, Notre Dame, UC Berkeley, Carnegie Mellon, Georgetown, UCLA, U.
Virginia, USC, U. Michigan, Tufts, UNC Chapel Hill, and NYU.
12. Presidential performance was evaluated based on criteria such as endowment
growth, admissions selectivity, alumni fund-raising participation, faculty
appointments, interviews with selected university trustees, and general reputation.

not-for-profit organization that supports health programs in poor communities worldwide, he has been recognized internationally for his work in the fight against HIV/AIDS and tuberculosis and for his efforts to bring quality health care to the world's impoverished.

Born in Seoul, South Korea, Kim is the first Asian American to be appointed president of an Ivy League institution. He came into the Hanover, New Hampshire, campus community with ambitious objectives: to challenge and inspire Dartmouth students to "make a difference in the world" by becoming more socially active change agents[13] and to position the college (which has the oldest medical school in the United States) to become a leader in transforming the delivery of health care. But before he could embark on this bold agenda, he had to perform some healing, particularly among the historically passionate and loyal alumni body.

Kim started at a fractious time in which the college's relations with its alumni were severely strained.[14] He worked smartly, embracing some of the college's most cherished institutions and winning support from the extended Dartmouth community. For example, Kim demonstrated to alumni, who had for years been battling the college over control of fraternities and funding for athletics, that he understands Dartmouth.

---

13. Kim frequently quotes John Sloan Dickey, Dartmouth's twelfth president, in challenging Dartmouth students to be more aware of the world outside of Hanover and to be citizens of the world. As Dickey said in his 1946 convocation address, "The world's troubles are your troubles . . . and there is nothing wrong with the world that better human beings cannot fix."

14. Alumni opposed efforts by former president James Wright to reduce the influence of fraternities at Dartmouth. The criticism escalated into legal action challenging the college's governance and costly campaigns waged by antagonists of the administration for election to the board of trustees.

YOU NEED A LEADER—NOW WHAT?

Contrary to what most people had expected, he *praised* the fraternities and sororities, emphasizing the strong bonds of friendship they foster rather than piling onto long-running criticism of how they propagate underage drinking. At the same time he initiated major new efforts to combat both binge drinking and sexual assault, in effect separating the problem behaviors from the long-standing cherished institutions that were only partially responsible for the problem.

He has been a visible supporter of the football team and the athletic program overall (Kim had been quarterback of his high school football team in Muscatine, Iowa, and also played basketball and golf). In late 2010, Kim won praise from the college sports community for recruiting Harry Sheehy, the athletics director of Williams College in Williamstown, Massachusetts, into the AD role at Dartmouth. In Sheehy's ten years at Williams, the college had won the award for having the top athletic program among the more than four hundred colleges that compose NCAA Division III. Kim is also instituting a speaker series modeled on the "Great Issues" class that had been taught at Dartmouth from 1947 to 1966. The course, which had been mandatory for seniors, brought speakers to campus to discuss civil rights, the Cold War, the space race, and other important topics of the day and is remembered fondly by many alumni from that era.

Kim knew that it would be impossible to achieve his ambitious goals without the active and beneficent support of Dartmouth's alumni. The early results have been encouraging. Kim closed an anonymous $35 million gift to found the Dartmouth Center for Health Care Delivery Science. The center will build on the work of the medical school where research has been undertaken into the causes of the disparity in the cost of delivering health care around the United States. Kim has said that Dartmouth should become the base of a new academic discipline, bringing researchers together to focus on health-care cost and quality. And for the Dartmouth class of 2015, applications, which are one of the most sensitive barometers of an institution's vibrancy, were up 15.7 percent, the second-largest increase in the Ivy League. Perhaps Kim's most significant accomplishment to date was the way he addressed the college's anticipated losses at the beginning of the economic downturn. Rather than using the endowment to fund significant operating losses, he took a very analytical, fact-based approach and aggressively attacked costs, procurement contracts, and administrative and faculty expenses and closed a $100 million operating deficit without raising the size of classes or adversely affecting the student experience.

Nonetheless, these are still early days for Kim in his presidential tenure. In Dartmouth he is leading a complex, multidimensional institution, which as was described in the chapter on the New York Public Library, is composed of a wide range of powerful and passionate stakeholders. Whether Kim can evolve into an enduringly "great" Dartmouth president, only time will tell. The fact remains that the college's trustees made a calculated bet on Kim's leadership potential, forgoing a president with proven prior experience in an identical role.

The experience of elite research universities hiring the sitting president of another large university has been less successful than when bringing in either the president of a smaller college or a provost or department chair from a comparable university. Here's an illustrative example of when a lateral leadership appointment didn't work out quite as planned at one of America's elite research universities.[15] A new president had been a renowned success story as president of another nationally recognized large research university. There, he had overseen a significant growth in the endowment from both investment returns and major gifts. He had recruited renowned scholars into the faculty. He had overhauled the university's athletic program, which has gone on to achieve national success in revenue-producing sports (football and basketball), while at the same time improving student-athlete graduation rates. However, in his first two years at his present university, according to several faculty members and trustees, there has been disappointment in the president's performance. He has come across as less energetic than his previous reputation and not up for the hard work of winning over the faculty on difficult issues. Although he had been a student at the university, he alienated faculty and alumni alike by referring to the governance model of his prior university as being "right" and "better."

First-time university presidents may be poised to outperform experienced presidents because of the all-consuming nature of these university leadership jobs today. A president who has proven herself in one institution often finds it challenging to perform at the same level in a new environment. Just as corporate leadership roles are becoming ever more challenging due

---

15. To maintain promised confidentiality, this particular "president" is actually a composite of several real individuals and how they transitioned from one major university to another.

to global competition, relentless technological change, shareholder activism, regulation, and the critical eye of the media and blogosphere, leaders in academic and other nonprofit organizations face all of these pressures and more. They face all the budgetary and organizational demands of a corporation and yet there are no P&Ls or share prices to function as a report card to grade performance and progress and incentivize performance. Then there are the constant pressures to raise money required to compete successfully for top faculty and students and build the facilities and programs that will attract and keep them. Student bodies are far more heterogeneous than they were in the past, which is obviously a huge positive, but their needs and interests are far more diverse, and as tuition costs continue to rise, the expectations of students and their parents are raised as well. And then there are the university trustees, powerful people who are simultaneously presidents' bosses and largest benefactors and who therefore necessitate enormous amounts of time and effort to cultivate and serve. Most challenging of all are the fiercely independent faculty members, who, with tenure and powerful faculty governance structures, make it especially challenging to drive change. Thus, most successful presidents figure out how to work effectively with faculty and gain support for investments whose benefit will accrue unevenly across schools and programs. Without faculty support, transformational change, which is so necessary for universities today, is challenging if not impossible.

Furthermore, the demands of a university presidency in terms of time and energy are not to be underestimated. There is no separation, for instance, between work and home since most presidents live on campus. Presidents have had to be so fully committed to their institution and the continuous work of building bridges with the numerous constituencies that if they are tapped to do it again at a comparable university, they have often lost the zeal that made them so successful the first time around. This is why only a minority of the top quartile of performers had previously been in the university president job. The emotional and intellectual commitment of first-time

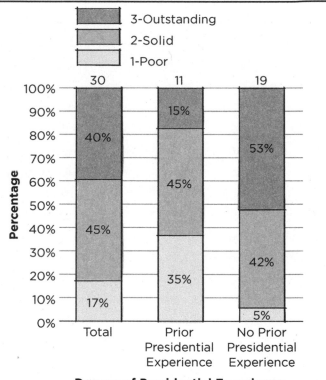

Performance and Presidential Experience

Degree of Presidential Experience

presidents to their institutions is often difficult for the experienced president to replicate.

The bottom line, whether in the corporate, educational, or nonprofit sector, is this: fail to challenge the seemingly logical assumption that direct prior experience in a comparable role is a prerequisite to success at your peril. Whether it is a question of companies, universities, or other organizations, the best experience may be one, two, or even three steps away from having "been there done that."

INDUSTRY EXPERIENCE

Another dimension of the experience question has to do with industry expertise. When making the choice about who should be appointed to key leadership jobs, one of the first questions that hiring managers and search committees wrestle with is whether industry experience is a "must-have" or a "nice-to-have." In some sectors (such as pharmaceuticals, technology, financial services, aerospace, and energy), many consider it next to impossible to succeed without having grown up in that industry. In these sectors, industry experience is widely accepted as a non-debatable leadership requirement when formulating position specifications. But how frequently do companies go outside of their industry for new leadership? What are the industry dynamics that make it possible or implausible for an industry outsider to succeed? Are there any industries when industry outsiders outperform industry-experienced executives? Answers to these questions will round out the potential red herring of experience.

Recall that outsiders were brought into the companies that composed our US and international research base approximately a quarter of the time. Of this group, three-quarters came from within the same industry or from adjacent industries and one-quarter were complete industry outsiders. As a proportion of all CEO appointments, only a mere 6 percent of these CEOs lacked any industry experience, whether direct or adjacent.

When analyzing performance, it turns out that there are no sectors in which industry outsiders as a group perform better than industry insiders. In one broad sector, diversified industrials, industry outsider performance has matched industry insiders. There are several others, including technology and pharma/biotech, that are so specialized there have been virtually no outsiders to analyze, while in others, such as retail and diversified industrial, a number of industry outsiders were appointed, suggesting that industry expertise has been considered a "nice-to-have." Here are the key factors underlying the top leadership dynamics in selected industries:

- In technology, companies face intense global competition and pricing pressure even while corporate spending recovers and consumer demand for technology-based products grows. In response, companies have launched dual-track strategies focusing on operational excellence to manage costs while also exploring new and potentially more profitable applications and products. The ever-accelerating convergence of entertainment, communications, and computing and the explosion of cloud computing have led to increasing demand for software, technical, and digital talent to manage the development of innovative products and services. These skills are very difficult to find in non-tech-industry-experienced executives.

• In pharmaceuticals and biotechnology, varied disciplines are coming together to open new frontiers in areas such as nanotechnology, genomics, proteomics, biodefense, and RNA research. A surge in venture capital investment, industry consolidation, and the drive to fortify pharmaceutical pipelines is fueling demand for experienced industry executives grounded in science. The largest pharmaceutical companies are walking a tightrope between the need to develop new blockbuster drugs to fill in product gaps due to expiring patents and demand from investors for double-digit returns. Given these challenges, pharmaceutical companies are demanding leaders with specialized backgrounds in drug development, commercialization, deal making, and industry operations to pursue the most cost-effective processes for developing the product pipeline, while balancing market, regulatory, and competitive demands. These skills are also considered next to impossible to find outside of pharmaceuticals and biotechnology.

• In retail, competition for consumer dollars has been greater than ever, and the incessantly competitive environment has created pricing pressures that require strict cost and inventory control. Retail companies require leaders who can examine every aspect of the business to streamline processes and costs. They also demand executives with marketing skills, financial acumen, technological expertise, and creativity necessary to capture market share. In some parts of retail, it is easier to generalize about the skills necessary to thrive in the industry—management experience with multilocation, real-estate-based, and online high transaction volume business models, which can be found outside of retail in restaurants, hospitality, rental cars, or even consumer banking. The major exception to considering generalized management talent for the retail industry, however, is when fashion-based apparel companies require design and merchandising expertise, unique to retailing, at the top.

- In the diversified industrial sector, the transformation brought about by technological advancements, global procurement, and international expansion has led to the need for executives with geographically diverse experience, as well as the financial know-how to run these complex companies. While exposure to and familiarity with the specific sector in question is important, industrial leaders generally need to be more talented general managers than industry experts. Clear-cut examples of this were Alan Mulally at Ford, as previously discussed, and Ed Whitacre at General Motors. Having served as chairman of the company for a mere three months before he took on the additional role of CEO, Whitacre demonstrated the adaptability to move to the manufacturing giant, switching from the telecommunications industry where he was the long-serving and high-performing CEO of AT&T and its predecessor company, SBC Communications. His general management and leadership skills honed from three decades at the top of a major, multinational company proved more important than his inexperience at an automaker. His successor, board member Dan Akerson, who was elected CEO of GM on August 11, 2010, on the eve of filing for its IPO, is also an industry outsider. Similar to Whitacre, Akerson's industry experience was in telecommunications, having served as chairman, chief executive officer, or president of several major companies, including General Instrument, MCI, Nextel, and XO Communications.

One way that companies requiring specialized industry expertise have fought against insularity, however, is by complementing industry insiders in the chief executive position with industry outsiders in the CFO role. Among Fortune 500 companies, those in the retail, communications/media/technology, and pharma/biotech industries—those which have shown the greatest proclivity to staying inside and in their own industries for the CEO—have appointed the greatest proportion of CFOs from *outside* the sector. In contrast, the diversified industrial sector, the one which has proven most able to accommodate high-performing industry outsiders in the CEO role, has been the one with the smallest proportion of industry outsiders in the CFO role.[16] This data underscores the broader point and one of the most important themes of this book. Organizational leadership is a team sport, not a solo activity.

---

16. According to Spencer Stuart's CFO Transition Study, over the 2004 to 2009 period, external industry CFO appointments have been as follows: Retail 65%, Communications/Media/Technology 52%, Pharma/Biotech 43%, and Industrial 30%; all other sectors fell between 31% and 42%.

ETHNICITY

You might think that Univision, the largest Spanish-language media company in the United States, would require Hispanic leaders—or at a minimum Spanish-speakers. But as CEO Joe Uva demonstrated, success can come in many languages. Uva's Spanish-language skills are those of a high school student who has taken a few courses. But he does know media and how to lead an organization. Most important, in the specific context of Univision, he had the sensitivity to and respect for the cultures of the company's diverse audience segments and employees that enabled him to overcome the obvious ethnic gap in his background.

When it comes to ethnocentric organizations, such as Hispanic-oriented Univision and Telemundo, or African American–focused BET, Radio One, and Essence Communications, the question of what is acceptable in terms of ethnicity for senior leaders is both delicate and important. As long as an otherwise highly qualified candidate has cultural sensitivity and respect for and understanding of other cultures, we believe that hiring managers should consider ethnicity as only one of the broader list of attributes that define who is the best leader to solve a situational puzzle.

While there have been financial and viewership losses for traditional broadcast networks, Univision has been building giant audiences, which increases its appeal to advertisers. In fact, in September 2010, Univision was the most popular network in the United States among viewers aged eighteen to forty-nine, the first time a Spanish-language station defeated CBS, ABC, Fox, and NBC in this key demographic. Although it's not clear that Uva would want the credit, it should be noted that this achievement occurred when some of Univision's tele-novelas (or soap operas that run five days a week), such as *Destilando Amor* (*Essence of Love*), were reaching the climaxes of their storylines. During Spain's 1–0 win over the Netherlands in the final of the 2010 World Cup in South Africa, for another example, Univision drew an audience in the United States of 8.8 million (which together with ABC's draw of 15.5 million combined to make this the most-watched soccer match ever in the United States with 24.3 million total viewers).

Uva, based in New York, was at the Univision helm from April 2007 through the end of his four-year contract in April 2011, dedicating much of his time to clients, actively work-ing with the advertising sales staff, and inspiring the company's different divisions to work closely together. Uva set a new tone at Univision, encouraging greater cross-company coopera-tion. For example, the broadcast and interactive programming reinforced each other, driving audiences to experience the company's content on multiple platforms. With his extensive background in media and marketing, Uva had been well aware of the opportunities presented by the Hispanic marketplace in the United States. In fact, in his previous role, as president and CEO of the media buying agency OMD Worldwide (a division of advertising company Omnicom), Uva helped create OMD Latino in 2004.

With his enthusiasm for and knowledge of the sector, it didn't matter that Joe Uva wasn't much of a Spanish-speaker.

And his leadership of the company didn't require a massive overhaul of the management, either. After carefully evaluating each executive, Uva replaced only three of the company's top fifteen executives and promoted some rising stars into top leadership roles, such as thirty-five-year-old Cesar Conde as president of Univision Networks. Uva also showed that the right person for a particular job was a function of the need coupled with the ability of the executive to be effective within the company's context rather than necessarily be Hispanic or even Spanish-speaking. For example, one of the key drivers of the company's growth has been English-speaking Kevin Conroy, who leads Univision's interactive division having made an excellent reputation at AOL for new product development and marketing over the course of a decade. The Univision board of directors chose to follow the Uva example once again in its leadership selection. In June 2011, Randy Falco, Univision's chief operating officer, who Uva had brought into the company after a long-serving NBC career and a stint as CEO of AOL, was named CEO.

Experience and the kind of personality that lends itself to becoming a strong cultural fit within an organization are simply more important than ethnicity when choosing a leader. Where someone is born, even what language someone speaks, should not necessarily restrict one's ability to fit in. A person's ability to understand a particular market and be an inspiring and effective leader can be universal.

IV.
USE THE
RIGHT PROCESS

7. A LEADERSHIP SELECTION
TALE OF TWO CITIES

We have now arrived at the third essential truth, using the right process in order to ensure the right leadership selection. The right process is composed of many discrete steps, which we will delve into in this section. An integral theme in pursuing the right process to choose the best person for a senior management position, however, is the importance of applying sound judgment to your deliberations. The very survival of your organization may be at stake.

That was certainly the case with an iconic American industrial giant founded nearly a century ago. Based in the Midwest of the United States, it has a proud history of product and process inventions. Its manufacturing innovations, management practices, and early commitment to employee safety have influenced the way business is done around the world today. Several years ago, however, after decades of market leadership, the company fell on hard times and "Joshua," its embattled CEO, was removed from his position by the board of directors.

An intense, intelligent, and soft-spoken man, Joshua had been well respected, even beloved in many parts of the organization. Starting with summer jobs in college, he worked his way up the ranks in sales, marketing, and general management across the company's divisions. After twenty-one years of service, he became chief operating officer and was appointed to the company's board of directors as well. Two years later he was promoted to chairman and CEO. Joshua was the living example of the company's values of hard work, honesty, loyalty, humility, a commitment to people, and engineering-led innovation.

Unfortunately, despite all these personal qualities, the company's situation under Joshua's watch became bleak. The company's leadership position had been eroded by intense competition in its primary markets from formidable Asian rivals that were undercutting its prices with lower labor costs and manufacturing in more modern plants. The company also overexpanded into capital-intensive new markets such as financial services and energy exploration. Serious questions had emerged about the company's strategy and portfolio of businesses. Growth had slowed and internal processes had bogged down decision making and new product development. As a consequence, employee morale was in a funk, and the company's share price had lost half of its value over the prior two years.

The company's board, dominated by a roster of directors with backgrounds from blue-chip companies, determined that it needed to replace Joshua and search for a new leader. On a Friday afternoon in October, the board publicly announced that it would seek a new CEO with "world-class industrial, manufacturing, and technical credentials, a dynamic, customer-focused orientation, and a record of achieving sustained growth running a diverse, global, multibillion-dollar company." The board of directors formed a search committee and charged it with scouring the world for candidates who best met these demanding criteria.

Joshua agreed to stay on the job while the search was under way. Nonetheless, the committee was under intense pressure to fill the leadership void as quickly as possible and literally worked every day on the search for ten weeks.[17] Within two weeks of the start of the search, they reviewed the backgrounds of approximately fifty prospective candidates from around the world and prioritized their dozen top choices to approach. Of these, they were able to develop five external candidates to interview, covering a wide range of industrial, automotive, and technology industry experiences. They had a viable and serious internal candidate as well. The committee winnowed the list to three finalists, two from the outside and one insider, and invited each for a three-hour conversation where they would have the opportunity to present and discuss their vision for the company.

The search committee conducted dozens of reference checks on each finalist, speaking with current and former colleagues, board directors, business leaders, industry analysts, and strategy consultants. Overall the feedback was positive, although there were a small number of contradictory opinions about the track records and strengths and weaknesses of each; most of the comments were highly positive, effusive even, but interspersed was a smattering of cautionary words. Pragmatically, the committee chalked up some of this "noise in the system" about the finalist candidates to the fact that anyone

---

17. Surprising as it today seems, it was not customary at the time for boards to appoint an interim chief executive during an emergency CEO succession. Nowadays, most boards have an emergency plan to install an interim CEO, which may be a board member, chief financial officer, general counsel, or other senior executive.

YOU NEED A LEADER—NOW WHAT?

leading a major company had to have developed some detractors along the way to the top. In addition, the overwhelming endorsement and supportive commentary from some of the most respected CEOs from corporate America gave the committee the confidence of their conviction in their final choice.

Less than three months after the launch of the search, a decision was reached and an announcement made that "Simon," the president and chief operating officer of a highly regarded diversified industrial conglomerate would become the new CEO. The board described Simon as being all about state-of-the-art manufacturing, industrial design, technology, marketing, and the customer. With his proven experience in emerging markets, he was introduced as "the person ideally suited to lead our great company forward."

The reaction to the announcement among the media, inside the company, and in the investment community was electric. A major exclusive story ran in *The Wall Street Journal*, the news lit up the wires from Asia and Europe to the company's campus headquarters, and the company's share price surged by over 5 percent. Simon brought energy, prestige, and pizzazz to the company. In his first week, he went around the world to meet with employees in town hall meetings and traveled with the sales force to meet the CEOs and top executives of the company's largest customers.

One priority from his earliest days was moving the internal culture away from warring tribes to getting people to deliver on a new vision of "integrated solutions" whereby the company's different businesses would be organized around major customers' needs rather than by the company's own products. Simon succeeded in getting the business units to be more collaborative, resulting in improved morale and customer satisfaction. He also visited the company's legendary product development and testing centers and was shown next-generation products that had been in development for three years. Simon implored the team to drop everything and rush one of the new products to market, which soon became a global industry phenomenon. On the CEO's two-year anniversary, the company's share price had increased by two-thirds; and in that same month, one of the major business magazines recognized him as one of the world's "Top 25 Business Leaders." The company was back, and there was a positive afterglow shining on all those who had a hand in bringing in a leader who seemed to revitalize the company so quickly.

Those first two years were literally "the best of times." But soon thereafter, the positive perceptions surrounding Simon started to change and the "worst of times" took hold. He became impatient with having to continually repeat why it was essential to change the company's deeply rooted culture. At the same time, Simon was the subject of magazine cover stories and a business cable network documentary about how "he" transformed the company from an old-line industrial manufacturer into a sophisticated fast-moving global technology giant. Employees came to resent Simon's high personal profile, and the culture started to revert to the fractious and insular organization that helped create the company's problems. What's more, Simon's biting public criticism of several members of the management team and his quips about how slow moving things were demoralized employees and began estranging him from the region's tightly knit business community as well. Equally significantly, so much of his and top management attention had been devoted to pushing the star new product out from the lab to the marketplace that R&D was deprived of resources. Consequently, there was little new in the product pipeline, making it difficult to sustain the company's momentum. To continue to grow the top line, the company was forced to deeply discount its most popular products, cutting into profit margins. Soon the formerly hit product was showing signs of weakness due to its saturation in the market and to newly emerging competitors that introduced similarly performing products at lower prices. At this point the company was on its back foot, momentum slowed, and its market share fell precipitously. With Simon's four-year contract coming due, the stress on his family from living in the icy Midwest far from their permanent home in the balmy Southeast, and feeling that "he had achieved the revitalization that he was hired to engineer," Simon announced his resignation.

What happened? What are the lessons learned from this corporate *Tale of Two Cities*?

With the benefit of hindsight, reflection, and interviews with all of the key protagonists, there is little doubt that along many dimensions Simon was the ideal fit with the company's situational jigsaw puzzle. At the same time, the very smart and committed people who led the search, including the selection committee, the external advisers, and full board, seemed to ignore a few telltale warning signs about their leadership selection. Also, when a business leader achieves tremendous success, such as was the case with Simon, with all the attendant external validation and plaudits, it is imperative for the individual, his advisers, and his board to keep him grounded.

One of the subtle warning signs may have had to do with the initial requirement that the candidate have a record of "sustained growth," by balancing the attainment of short-term objectives with investing for the long term. At his prior company, Simon, working as part of the leadership team consisting of himself as COO, a chairman and CEO, and a CFO, achieved eighteen consecutive quarters of revenue and profit growth. However, when the economy tanked at the start of the millennium, the company's quarterly revenues slid by 20 percent the first year and by a further 25 percent the second year. Market share fell from 22 percent one year to 13 percent the next year as less expensive competitive products hit the market. The company's stock price plunged 95 percent. Of course, this free fall was not all that different from that experienced by other industrial giants whose fortunes also declined as a result of the economic bust. In retrospect, it was clear that Simon was more of a growth leader, where it is more possible to deliver both quarter-to-quarter sales and profit goals *and* make important investments, than a turnaround manager, who is effective at making the tough trade-offs between the short and long terms.

When he assumed the CEO post, according to several former executives who worked with him, Simon limited the investment in R&D and channeled the company's resources into shorter-term priorities. Rather than continuing to invest in groundbreaking products and services, he acquired companies in different industry sectors and poured further billions of dollars into stock buybacks in order to drive the stock price in the short term.

There was a long list of personal characteristics that rounded out the committee's key selection criteria for which Simon proved to be a strong match. He certainly brought high energy, intellectual prowess, a passion for world-class design, a desire to win in the marketplace, and outstanding communications skills. But there were two attributes that were not on the list that in retrospect should have been: a fact-based, operationally oriented decision maker; and the ability to thrive under pressure. When it came to operational decisions, Simon seemed to focus less on data and analysis than on the opinions of a very tight circle of executives he listened to. He was also inclined, according to one former company executive, "to follow the latest management fad among CEOs at the Business Roundtable."

By year three of Simon's tenure, the cash generated from all but eliminating R&D spending was becoming a hoard on the company's balance sheet, despite the company's sputtering performance. This made the company a tempting target to activist investors. Specifically, it attracted the interest, ire, and investment of one of the most visible corporate raiders, who launched a heated campaign to gain three board seats, remove the company's management, force a massive stock buyback, and split the company in three. According to a number of former company executives and board directors, Simon "became a different CEO" when this heat was turned on. He became fixated on what the corporate raider and the business media said publicly; and privately this seemed to preoccupy him. The

CEO's former decisiveness turned into tentativeness, and he bent under the pressure of the investors' demands. By all appearances, the CEO found it difficult to set and stay on a winning course of getting the right products developed and into the market and making money while adapting to the challenging new competitive and investor reality.

During the search process, a couple of issues were not probed as deeply as would have been ideal. Remember the dozens of references, almost all of which were positive? There were two questions raised by individuals who knew Simon well, wondering first how he would react when the stress level of the job rose into the red zone, and whether his decision making was too driven by PR and Wall Street. In the rush to fill the leadership void, the search committee rationalized the questions as outliers, potential issues to be managed, perhaps, but far outweighed by the sea of positive commentary. In retrospect, of course, the concerns expressed were justified. One person, almost as an aside, mentioned Simon as "not having been around when the business went down the drain" at his prior company.

The key lesson is not only that following the right process demands doing proper due diligence, but that it is just as essential to exercise the judgment and discipline to prioritize the streams of information coming in to draw fact-based conclusions. Putting it another way, focus more on the issues raised in references than on the positives. Not that anyone should be held to a standard of perfection. But when the inevitable limitations, weaknesses, or concerns arise, it is imperative to probe them deeply and assess whether or not they cut to the core of the situation at hand, which must be carefully diagnosed up front. In reflecting on the lessons learned from this *Tale of Two Cities,* one of the members of the search committee recently told us, "Every major mistake about choosing a new leader, whether a CEO or otherwise, can be traced to insufficient due diligence and misjudging how the information we learned fit into the context into which we were hiring." Indeed, it could be just a few negative "flecks" floating in a sea of positives that in the end constitute a candidate's Achilles' heel in your particular situation.

In any case, despite the stellar early ride and the renewed momentum, pride, and prestige brought back into the company, the record indicates that Simon was not able to carry the company through to the success that the company and surely he himself desired. Perhaps in the end, those who chose the CEO (and the CEO himself) who got the choice wrong could have avoided the mistake by combining better due diligence with the power of constituency interviews.

8. THE POWER OF CONSTITUENCY INTERVIEWS

Ask and you shall receive. When it comes to the art of leadership broadly speaking and the specific application of establishing a leadership selection process, this age-old saying holds a lot of truth. When good questions are posed in the right way, the best answers emerge. People can make decisions for themselves, and complex problems, such as how to secure buy-in for a new leadership choice, can be solved with elegance.

When choosing a person for a top position, the first step in setting an organization on the path to success is the *constituency interview*. Remember that making the right leadership choice is not just about finding a "great" individual; it's about solving an intricate and dynamic jigsaw puzzle. Constituency interviews can be a powerful diagnostic technique for achieving this goal by creating a shared understanding of the situation. They create buy-in in terms of what an organization is looking for in its leadership and can unify even a divisive organization. This buy-in then helps set up a leader for success, whether promoted from within or recruited from outside.

What follows are examples of two different situations: one in which the designated heir-apparent conducted the constituency interviews himself; the second was conducted by those responsible for a search.

KEVIN SHARER JOINED AMGEN, the giant biotech company, as president and chief operating officer in October 1992 and became its CEO in May 2000. As the designated heir-apparent, Sharer had about a year between being named the next CEO and officially assuming the title, so he had plenty of time to build a support base. "I don't care how long you've been in a company," he told us. "You don't just show up and tell everybody how it's going to be. Especially when you're promoted from within to become the boss, you have to earn people's respect in the new role." The most important thing he did when appointed CEO was to ask questions to create an environment where he and, by extension, the company really listened. How Sharer did this illustrates one proven approach for constituency interviews.

The very day in December 1999 when Amgen announced that he would become CEO, Sharer sent out a memo to more than a hundred director-level-and-above staff at the company, saying he would be scheduling one-on-one meetings with each of them. Sharer framed the meetings around five questions:

1. What are the three most important things about Amgen we should be sure to preserve and why?

2. What are the top three things we need to change and why?

3. What do you most hope I do?

4. What are you most concerned I might do?

5. What advice do you have for me?

Sharer spent an hour with each executive, listening to the commentary stimulated by these open-ended questions. He says that he had to use self-restraint to remain quiet and let people talk. And once they started talking, the information poured out. He filled yellow pad after yellow pad with notes. When he was finished with the first hundred sessions, he analyzed and synthesized the results and communicated them across the company through "Listening Memos" and presentations. These then became the basis for shaping his actions and decisions throughout his first year as chief executive.

In addition to providing the input for what became his strategic agenda for the company, Sharer says that the process helped garner buy-in for his program. Why? People appreciate being asked their views and genuinely listened to, regardless of whether their specific points of view are implemented.

SIMILARLY, THE BOARD of the Public Broadcasting Service, popularly known as PBS, used constituency interviews during its search for a new leader in the fall of 2005. Founded in 1969, PBS is a not-for-profit organization with 349 member stations across the United States. The broad range of constituency interviews was unprecedented in our experience, but they were necessary to understand and gain consensus among a diverse and extended network of stakeholders as well as the complex and powerful forces at work surrounding public broadcasting at a time of upheaval in the media, technology, and political environment.

Over a three-month period, from September to December 2005, more than one hundred constituency interviews, some in person, some by telephone, were conducted. Every member of the PBS search committee, current and former board members, the senior management staff in Washington, producers of public broadcasting content, other nonprofit media organizations, current individual and corporate donors, the Corporation for Public Broadcasting (the congressionally mandated funder of public broadcasting), even on-air talent were all part of this interview process. These stakeholder interviews were intended to serve two purposes:

1. To gather insight, advice, and recommendations to help guide the search committee as far as the requirements for the PBS president

2. To build a body of knowledge and input from the public broadcasting community to help the next PBS president get off to a fast and effective start when appointed

Beyond the issues about PBS's transformation to the digital world, interview topics included challenges to the PBS funding model and the centrifugal forces diverging the interests of different categories of member stations (e.g., large-market stations like WGBH in Boston, WETA in Washington, DC, and KQED in San Francisco; small-market stations such as WMEB of Bangor, Maine; and university stations like WTIU of Bloomington, Indiana). In the end, the process helped create the foundation on which the new CEO would be set up for success.

Taking a page from Sharer's stakeholder interviews when he became CEO of Amgen, the PBS constituency interviews were also based on five questions, carefully constructed to elicit constructive input rather than a litany of complaints. Specifically, the first question, "What about PBS needs to be preserved and why?," was designed to have people start their discussions with the positive attributes about the organization.

1. **What about PBS needs to be preserved?** The themes about what needed to be preserved were consistent across the interviews: maintaining PBS's structure as a membership organization constructed as a local (member station)–national (PBS) partnership; PBS's programming excellence in culture, public affairs, and children's programming; and its commitment to its education and public service roots. These were considered central to maintaining the loyalty of and interconnection with PBS's audiences, its journalistic integrity, and the distinctiveness of the PBS brand.

   After emphasizing the positive aspects of the organization and what needed to be protected, the constituency interviews then shifted to what the organization and by extension the new leader needed to address in the future.

2. **What about PBS needs to change?** Three areas formed the core about what needed to be improved. First was to achieve greater clarification and alignment of roles between PBS and the different types of member stations. PBS did not produce programming; it commissioned content from major producing stations, such as WGBH or WNET in New York. But it was important for smaller-market stations to influence the national programming strategy as well. Second, PBS's business model, which was heavily reliant on fund-raising by individual member stations rather than from having its own endowment, put continuous pressure on member stations to do pledge drives. When PBS wanted to build its capital base and do fund-raising on a national level, it was essential to balance it with local efforts. The third theme about what needed to change was to improve PBS's organizational effectiveness to enable it to adjust to the rapidly changing media and technology competitive environment.

Flowing logically and directly from these two interview topics, the next area probed in the constituency interviews was what this all implied for the leadership requirements for the next PBS leader.

3. **What are the most important characteristics and experience for the next PBS leader?** The common themes that emerged from this question had to do with the leader having an understanding of the public broadcasting system and its history, proven fund-raising

expertise; an understanding of television programming and relevant technology; leading by example; and being a diplomat with strong influencing skills. As one stakeholder said, "We need a candidate who can bring the system together."

The next question asked for specific candidate nominations.

4. **Who do you recommend as a candidate to lead PBS?** There were over fifty nominations generated by the constituency interviews, with the number of mentions tabulated for the committee's consideration. Finally, each stakeholder was offered an open-ended catchall question to provide input into the process, and in so doing reinforced the buy-in bestowed into the process.

5. **What is your advice for the committee?** Here stakeholders urged that the process be conducted swiftly to help the organization move forward decisively in such a rapidly changing environment. The PBS board was also urged to clarify the extent to which it was a modern media company focusing on increasing audience share or a membership organization dedicated to making its member stations strong. It was also advised to be prepared to pay more money to attract the right leader.

AN IMPORTANT BENEFIT to weaving the constituency interview approach into your leadership selection process is that you can literally hand over the write-up from the interviews to the new leader once the selection process is completed. In January 2006, Paula Kerger, chief operating officer of WNET/13 in New York, was unanimously elected to become the new CEO of PBS. Following her appointment, she was given a 125-page report, which accelerated her learning about the strategic priorities and hot-button issues, saving what would have taken her months of fieldwork to accomplish.

Over her six-plus years as CEO, Kerger has followed much of the guidance provided by the constituency interview process. She has led PBS to expand the ways that its audience can access content. It has expanded its content to span multiple platforms, including moving video programming online for web streaming and building social networking and interactive tools on its site, PBS.org. It has experimented with seeking out viewers for the PBS website through online tags and search engine optimization. Kerger has said that PBS has long been a pioneer in media, being the first, for example, to utilize closed captioning and a national satellite. Today PBS distributes its content on platforms such as Xbox and Hulu. Thanks to the constituency interviews, the PBS leadership selection process contributed directly to the success of Paula Kerger as CEO.

9. WHEN TO USE A HORSE RACE

You've established your strategic priorities and leadership requirements and completed your constituency interviews. You've also invested the time and effort to develop several potentially viable alternative leaders for an important position. Now you confront the question of how to put the candidates through their paces in order to evaluate which one is best. But you have to decide how explicitly you want to set up the competition and how public you want to make the process. Otherwise said, Do you set up a horse race to select your new leader?

Let's dig into this question now.

General Electric has long been recognized for excellence and best practices in the art of management. So back in 1999 and 2000 during its widely publicized horse race between Jeff Immelt, Bob Nardelli, and Jim McNerney to become the successor to Jack Welch, many people came to see this process as the best way for their companies to select a CEO. After all, GE did it this way; and it was logical—putting the best candidates through a rigorous testing and evaluation process, seeing who performed the best, and picking the winner to get the job. Now over a decade later, however, many people involved in people leadership decisions recognize the risks of running a derby. While elements of a competitive selection process clearly bring out the best in candidates—think of a lump of coal undergoing sustained pressure and coming out a diamond—if not managed carefully, it can also bring out the dark side of interpersonal behavior and corporate politics.

A horse race is an explicit succession process that takes place over a predetermined time frame in which at least two internal candidates are put through a series of assessments and activities in order to decide who will be chosen as the organization's next leader. The process may be done quietly or quite visibly, as in the case of GE or more recently at Procter & Gamble, unfolding in the glare of the media and investment community.

At P&G it was widely reported in the business press that the race to succeed CEO A. G. Lafley was between Susan Arnold, president of the company's global business units, and Robert McDonald, the company's chief operating officer. Investment analysts who follow P&G were like CIA Kremlinologists evaluating the May Day military parades of the now defunct Soviet Union, searching for clues as to who was in the lead. After P&G's presentations to analysts in 2009, for example, Sanford C. Bernstein analyst Ali Dibadj commented that "there was a most clear push of momentum to Bob McDonald that the company was trying to signal to the Street. McDonald had given a broad overview of the company's plans to expand and cut costs, whereas Susan Arnold took a step back and did a sustainability presentation," reviewing how "green" P&G was managing its business. Clearly, assigning the strategic overview to McDonald had all the markings of designating him as the next leader as strategy falls squarely in the realm of the CEO. This prognostication turned out to be spot-on. The succession race narrowed with the

March 2009 exit of Arnold, clearing the way for rival McDonald to emerge as the leader of the world's biggest consumer-products company. He assumed the president and CEO post on July 1, 2009.

A horse race that plays out confidentially, under the radar with minimal external and even internal visibility, has significant advantages over a public gladiatorial spectacle. In fact, a rigorous, fair, and transparent process implemented with sufficient confidentiality to minimize organizational jockeying has the dual advantage of potentially arriving at the right decision and adding value along the way. We'll call this carefully planned competitive succession situation a "fail-safe horse race." At "Major Global Inc.," a multibillion-dollar company in the technology and business services industry, a special committee of the board, supported by the incumbent CEO and the chief human resources officer, established a virtual gauntlet of activities that the company's three most senior operating executives were put through. Over a twelve-month period, each candidate was evaluated by executive assessment specialists, built a development plan with the help of an executive coach to address the feedback from the assessments, met individually with all board directors to discuss their operating units and the future of the business, assumed management responsibility for a specific cross-functional corporate initiative, developed a vision and strategy for the company and how they would lead it as CEO, and made a formal presentation of their vision and plan to the full board. We'll see how Major Global's "fail-safe" horse race played out in the succession process (see pages 155–183).

In addition to enabling the board to make a fact-based assessment for selecting its new leader, these steps proved to be an important development opportunity for the three executives. They were battle tested and given broadening experiences. They were each also given the gift of in-depth feedback, an increasingly rare phenomenon as people move higher into the senior ranks. The horse race is similar to an election campaign as candidates become accustomed to, and able to deal with, the glare of internal and potentially external scrutiny to prepare them for the real thing.

Those are the positive aspects of a horse race. The downside is that it creates visible winners and losers. "Obviously it was competitive between the three of us," one of the internal candidates at Major Global said, "and we didn't know what would happen at the end. But we all bought into the process." It is often the case where the losers leave the company, as happened when Bob Nardelli went to Home Depot and Jim McNerney went to 3M in the immediate aftermath of Jeff Immelt's selection at GE. A horse race can also become distracting to the organization, politicizing it with counterproductive water-cooler speculation and camps developing to support one candidate over others. Furthermore, during the process, successes and gaffes often take on disproportionate importance, outweighing years or decades of performance.

So if you are in the enviable situation of having two or three viable internal succession candidates, how do you make a horse race a "fail-safe" one and benefit from its advantages while mitigating the risks? First, design a rigorous process and be clear with each of the participants about how it will unfold and over what period of time. Second, emphasize that the process is just as important as the end result, particularly that the company is investing in the development of each candidate. Third, consider locking in the protagonists through retention compensation strategies and additional management responsibilities and ensuring that once chosen, the new leader quickly reaches out to executives who lost the race as well as key members of their teams. And finally, continually assess how the insiders are stacking up against the best outside talent, recognizing that any potential external candidate will have to have significantly better experience to justify the risks of going outside.

We will delve into the details of the process with Major Global. But first we will address the other essential part of the right leadership selection process, how to structure candidate interviews.

10. ORCHESTRATING
CANDIDATE INTERVIEWS

How do you and your organization present your best face
to top-level candidates and develop a thorough, accurate
portrait of their ability to thrive in your team's unique culture?
By orchestrating candidate interviews with care.

In this chapter we'll present twelve guidelines for successful candidate interviews and then look at how the New York
Public Library presidential search committee structured interviews of the different candidates.

1. **Details count**. In an executive interviewing process,
   the earliest contacts, including how candidates are
   treated when an interview is scheduled and the materials
   are provided in advance of the meeting, help set a positive tone with them. When interviewing outsiders, some
   companies, for example, send product samples to a candidate's home before the interview to bring the company
   to life. Every interaction with a candidate, from the re-
   ceptionist's greeting to the choreography in between interview appointments, communicates the organization's
   professionalism and interest in the candidate.

2. **Select interviewers carefully**. The appropriate mix
   of interviewers depends on the position and to whom

it reports. In general, it is valuable to have individuals who will interact regularly with the successful candidate. Some situations call for including peers or future direct reports in the interview process. However, think carefully about potentially delicate situations, such as giving potential future direct reports veto power over their future boss's hiring. The best interviewers embody the culture of the organization, have a good eye for talent, and display the energy and enthusiasm that will resonate with candidates. Ideally, a core group of interviewers meet with all of the candidates for a particular position or level within the organization.

3. **Coordinate interviews.** Interviewers should have assigned areas of focus for their meetings with a candidate. A coordinated approach allows interviews to collectively cover broader territory and learn the most they can about the candidate. Minimize the duplication of questions by assigning to each interviewer specific areas or topics to probe. Ideally bring interviewers together for a brief meeting prior to the interviews to discuss their respective roles. Finally, interviewers should be diligent about posing the same set of questions to each candidate. A coordinated approach is not only effective for garnering valuable information, it also communicates to the candidate that the company is organized, efficient, and dedicated to high quality.

4. **Be focused, timely, and polite.** Make sure to set aside an appropriate amount of time for the meeting, and do

not allow interruptions. Be on time, and schedule interviews with the flexibility to run longer if the conversation warrants it. Understand that senior-level candidates are not like college or graduate school students interviewing on campus. They are busy professionals who are interested in pursuing the opportunity, but are nonetheless sacrificing their time to interview.

5. **Plan your questions**. Come prepared to the interview. Review the candidate's résumé carefully. Develop some predetermined questions that are tailored to the requirements of the position and that link with the candidate's background. Be sure to get quickly to the heart of the discussion. When candidates have to repeat basic information included in their résumé or spend a lot of time discussing mutual acquaintances, valuable time is taken away from the core discussions about the requirements of the position and the mutual fit. Here are five questions that have proved useful in analyzing whether the candidate is a potential good fit into an organization's jigsaw puzzle.

- Describe in detail a working environment you've experienced where you felt most effective and happiest.

- If I had an opportunity to speak candidly with your boss, without any concern about confidentiality, what would I hear? How would this differ from what your friends would say?

- Using three adjectives, describe the ideal operating culture in which you thrive and why.

- If you were to leave your organization today and a dinner was held to honor you for your service, how would you be roasted? What lasting accomplishment would be most mentioned?

- What do you find most energizing and motivating about your current role? What activities are most frustrating and cause you to procrastinate?

6. **Listen thoughtfully.** Senior-level candidates tend to be skilled interviewers and engaging personalities, so it is important to concentrate on getting the answers needed to understand their capabilities and weaknesses as they pertain to the role. Listen thoughtfully to their responses, including the way they answer questions and the quality of their thought processes. Resist the temptation to do too much of the talking, and don't be afraid of silent pauses. As a general rule, the candidate should do three-quarters of the talking.

7. **Assess cultural fit.** Use your time with candidates to understand how they may fit in with the organization's personalities, internal dynamics, and culture. Ask specific questions that get at the individual's communication and interpersonal styles and temperament. Questions that require candidates to illustrate how they have accomplished specific tasks in past roles can help reveal their leadership

style, including their approach to working in teams, sensitivity to internal politics, and openness to others' opinions.

8. **Encourage and answer the tough questions.** Don't shy away from asking candidates direct questions about issues in their background or their management or communication style. Avoiding sensitive topics during the interview could set both the company and the candidate up for problems later. Similarly, be honest about the realities of the position and the company's challenges. Savvy candidates have done their homework, and most are likely to be aware of many of the issues confronting the organization. Discussing the challenges and the company's approach to dealing with them in a straightforward manner will increase your and your organization's credibility with the candidate and importantly avoid mis-setting expectations should he or she accept the position. Here are five of the best questions that candidates could ask to gain insight into your culture and environment:

- In one or two sentences, how would you describe your culture?

- Tell me about a successful hire that has worked well in your culture. What is it about them or their personal style that has enabled them to thrive? Describe someone who didn't work out and why.

- What are the biggest surprises, either positive or negative, that new senior executives face when they join your company?

- What do you like best about the organization and what still needs to change?

- Describe the style and behaviors of one of your top performers who left the company. Why is he or she no longer with you?

9. **Sell the opportunity**. Talented candidates often have many options from which to choose and want to work for the best organizations that have the brightest futures in roles that give them a stake in achieving important goals. Seize the opportunity to show your personal passion and deliver a compelling message about future plans and opportunities for the organization.

10. **Follow up after the interview**. One of the key decision makers should contact the candidate following the interview. A personal call or e-mail to a candidate thanking him or her and sharing any afterthoughts is almost always received very positively.

11. **Collect feedback**. Circle back with your fellow interviewers to gather feedback while thoughts are fresh. This both ensures that assessments are more accurate and keeps the process moving by enabling prompt feedback to the candidate. Some companies convene a short roundtable meeting at the end of an interview day to share observations. In a debriefing session, allow each person to briefly share views about the candidate's fit with the role and the organization or prepare an easy-to-complete feedback form. One point of caution: the

order in which observations are shared can influence the views or comments of others. To promote the most open and honest assessments, have the most senior executives share their opinions last.

12. **Maintain candidates' confidentiality**. Even when motivated by the best of intentions, when it comes to external candidates, the interview team should resist the temptation to reach out to contacts at an individual's current or former organization for information. Word that someone is interviewing tends to spread quickly, potentially creating serious problems for the candidate. Conduct background checks and thorough referencing at the appropriate time in the process and in a discreet manner.

ORGANIZATIONS THAT ARE the most successful at recruiting consider the interviewing process from the candidate's perspective. They treat candidates respectfully in all phases of the process and are responsive, decisive, open, and attentive. They balance their responsibility to accurately assess the candidate's fit for the role with the ability to understand, package, and sell the strengths and opportunities of the company.

NYPL REDUX

The New York Public Library search committee understood that first-round interviews are more effective when focused on the specifics of what candidates have accomplished and how they approached and addressed challenges throughout their careers. Philosophical or forward-looking questions, such as "What is your definition of leadership?" or "Where do you see yourself in ten years?," do not help predict how people will behave in organizational leadership roles. Visioning exercises and other such future-oriented topics are better left for later in the process. It is important in early interviews to ask for actual examples about critical situations and how candidates handled them. When the interview is concluded, you should then have a very good sense of the situations candidates have faced, how they have behaved, what actions they took, and what the results were.

The eight critical competencies and position responsibilities for the NYPL presidency and the corresponding candidate interview questions were as follows:

1. *Transformational leadership and vision*: The New York Public Library is a large and complex institution with a commitment to public access, education, and research, and a history of building world-class collections. We are seeking a leader who can enhance and build upon our commitment to and implementation of this mission, perhaps in new and innovative ways. Please tell us about your experience in crafting a distinctive leadership positioning for your organization—one that built upon its strengths or transformed it in concrete ways to ensure its relevance and improve its effectiveness. How did you align your staff with your strategy and vision and deal with opposition to your plan?

2. *Leadership and management*: We require a strong leadership team and talent at all levels of the organization. Please tell us how you have organized your senior leadership team, how you work and communicate with them, and your experience in acquiring talent for your organization.

3. *Diversity*: A significant strength of the New York Public Library lies in its value of maintaining and nurturing a diverse and multicultural workforce and a continuing commitment to diversity at all levels. What efforts have you taken to ensure that diversity plays an important and productive role in your organization? What challenges did you face and how did you go about resolving them?

4. *The role of technology*: We expect that you have thought about the role of technology and digitization as it relates to libraries, learning, and the distribution of information. Please share with us examples in which you utilized a technology agenda to solve organizational problems, improve the delivery of products and/or services, or to transform a fundamental aspect of your organization's mission and strategy?

5. *Resource development*: The New York Public Library has a complex funding model that requires governmental support as well as substantial support from a group of generous private donors. Please share with us your experiences in acquiring and developing resources for your organization including work with government, foundations,

corporate sponsors, and private donors. Please be as specific as possible.

6. *Scholarly values and community service*: At NYPL you would be asked to lead and balance the institution's commitment to community service and scholarship. Please tell us about some experiences you have had in which dual and sometimes competing missions were in play, how you approached each constituency, and how you addressed the needs of each while moving the institution forward.

7. *Advocacy and public presence*: As the president of the New York Public Library, you would serve as its primary advocate and public voice to a wide range of constituents— patrons; local, state, and federal officials; donors and supporters; the intellectual community of scholars, writers, and librarians; and the media. We would like to learn more about your experience serving as the public face and voice of an organization. Please tell us about some of your experiences in dealing with the public and the press. We would appreciate hearing about a strategic public advocacy plan and one that was difficult and challenging.

8. *Board experience and relationships*: The NYPL Board of Trustees is a major source of philanthropic support and the fiduciary responsible for ensuring the long-term health of the institution. So the relationship between the president and the board is critical. Have you had experience as

a board member and as an executive reporting to a board of trustees? Please share with us some of your experiences in working with your board to develop strategies for your organization. How did you work with your chair to align your interests and plans? If there was an occasion in which you and your board chair disagreed, how did you resolve the issue?

WITH THESE QUESTIONS SET, the search committee was able to delve deeper into candidates' actual capabilities and accomplishments as they related to what all the constituency interviews showed as the major priorities. They were then able to continue evaluating candidates, which ranged from college and university presidents and chief librarians, to top digital media executives, as the search progressed.

V.
PUTTING IT
ALL TOGETHER

11. THE CASE OF MAJOR GLOBAL

et us now illustrate what a comprehensive process looks like that applies everything we've covered so far through the real-life example of Major Global Incorporated,[18] a leading American technology and business services company with $15 billion in revenues.

Roger, the current chief executive of Major Global, is sixty-four years old. He has spent his entire career with the company, rising through sales, operations, and general management positions, becoming chief operating officer about ten years ago. He has served as a board director at two public companies, one a large utility and the other a major aerospace company. Roger had been promoted to CEO by the Major Global board five years ago without a rigorous succession process. Although it all worked out well in the end, Roger knew that this was not only a risky way to choose a CEO but that in today's governance environment it would expose the board to criticism or even shareholder lawsuits.

Five years ago the then CEO, who was sixty-three years old, in good health and performing well over the nine years that he was in the job, dropped the bombshell that he had decided to retire in two months. To say that this caught the

---

18. Major Global is a pseudonym for a leading American technology and business services company, and names and other details have been disguised.

board by surprise is an understatement. While they had gone through the motions of discussing succession once a year, it was never a central topic of a board meeting. And other than Roger, who as chief operating officer and a corporate director had been coming to board meetings for years, the board really didn't know any other members of the senior management team. So when the incumbent recommended that they promote Roger—"He's earned the job"—the board went right along. Not only was it a logical decision, but there was no immediate alternative. And though they didn't verbalize it, no one on the board wanted to be seen as having been unprepared. They knew that CEO succession was supposed to be their number one responsibility. There was no one more surprised about the sequence of events than Roger himself. He had been given no forewarning by the retiring CEO, and he was promoted that same day without any discussions, much less interviews, with the board. He knew that he wanted the job, he had been pointing toward it his entire career, and over the last few years he always believed it was a matter of when, not if. But still, the abruptness of the appointment somehow felt hollow to Roger.

Roger vowed then and there that when it was time for him to hand over the keys, he would not let it just happen nonchalantly. He would do everything in his power to ensure the best and most rigorous process. This time the board certainly agreed, because the context in which it dispatched its governance responsibilities was starkly different. Even though Roger's appointment as CEO took place just five years earlier, much had changed with the way leadership selection is done. With more than eight years since the passage of Sarbanes-Oxley legislation, boards have definitively wrested control of CEO succession away from incumbent chief executives. Today, boards are both more proactive about and simply better at leadership succession. They have come to realize they can't afford to be caught flat-footed by a crisis, whether it be the CEO stepping down without notice, being recruited away, or being forced to resign in scandal.

Boards, including that of Major Global, want to get ahead of potential problems. From the start of Roger's tenure as CEO they decided to make leadership succession a standing agenda item at all board meetings, and once a year Roger, the company's chief human resources officer, and the chairman of the board compensation committee led a deep-dive talent review for the full board. Also, over the course of the year, each board member spent one-on-one time with the top five company executives; and on a rotating schedule across the year, the most promising up-and-comers in the company were given an opportunity to present to the board.

In mid-2009, Roger shared with the board that when he turned sixty-five (eighteen months hence), he wanted the company to be in a position to have a successor named. So he asked the chairman of the compensation committee to lead a process that would ensure that this came to be. The passion and commitment of Roger and the entire board to do the search for his successor the right way energized everyone involved.

The process was structured into six steps.

STEP 1—COMPANY SITUATION ASSESSMENT

During its annual offsite strategy meeting, the board discussed the key leadership requirements for the company's next leader. The management team prepared an assessment of the current state of the business and a likely picture of the company five years in the future. The key principle is assessing whether the skills and experiences of the candidates were what Major Global needed to meet its future challenges. What the board was trying to do was avoid "driving by looking at the rearview mirror"—that is, assuming that the skills required by the company for success in the past would be those needed for the future. The board was able to use insights gained from the CEO Transition Study, particularly the importance of choosing a CEO not only with great skills but with those that were in sync with the situation of the company.

CURRENT STATE OF THE COMPANY AND BUSINESS

Understanding the current state of the business was therefore essential, and here is how the management team summarized it for the board:

- Revenue $15 billion growing more rapidly than the industry

- Profitability at record levels

- International with businesses in many countries operating fairly autonomously

- Independent business units well established in their respective industry sectors; in the process of reassessing organizational and P&L boundaries

- Searching for adjacent business opportunities to sustain growth

- Internally focused culture and slow in decision making

LIKELY FUTURE STATE OF THE COMPANY
AND BUSINESS

Through scenario planning, the management team presented what they believed represented a realistic and appropriately ambitious likely future state of the business five years out:

- Revenue $20+ billion

- Portfolio restructuring: slow-growth business units in mature market spun off and new businesses acquired in multiple geographies

- Rapid growth in emerging markets, particularly China, Brazil, and India, and a more integrated global business model

- Adjacent business opportunities captured through organic growth and more aggressive M&A

- New opportunities characterized by greater regulatory requirements and interdependencies

- More diverse distribution channels, e.g., direct and indirect sales, online

- A more externally focused organization with increased emphasis on marketing and customer solutions

NEW CEO'S CHALLENGES

As part of the situation analysis, the management team detailed what it believed would be the major challenges that the next CEO would confront in the first two years of his or her tenure:

- Developing and driving a coherent growth strategy; balancing growth and cost-reduction in resource allocation and investment decisions

- Earning the respect of the organization

- Building the management team, attracting and retaining top talent

- Managing and prioritizing the diversity and complexity of businesses and issues faced

- Evolving the company's culture into a faster, more decisive organization

- Developing effective relationships with board members

- Earning credibility and building relationships with the investor community

STEP 2—BUILDING CEO CANDIDATE PROFILE

Given the current and projected future states of the business as well as the next CEO's near-term challenges, the management team and board debated, iterated, and ultimately agreed on the key requirements for the new CEO. They determined that five broad areas of experience and personal characteristics would be the road map to identify and evaluate potential candidates (both internal and external).

1. General Management Experience and Track Record of Consistent Successful Results in a Business-to-Business Sector

   - Experience having run a portfolio of businesses with a global footprint

   - Success managing through different business cycles

   - Experience in driving new business growth through a large direct sales force

2. Technology Expertise

   - Experience managing systems and platform consolidations

   - Digital savvy and an understanding of the impact of cloud computing on service delivery

3. Mergers and Acquisitions Experience

- Track record of managing significant acquisitions from target identification through negotiation and closing

- Experience in postmerger integration

4. Global Experience

- Responsibility for multicountry businesses that are ideally global in nature

- Ideally, experience having lived in multiple countries

- Cultural sensitivity—the ability to relate well to different cultures

5. Inspiring Leadership and Personal Characteristics

- The ability to attract and develop strong teams and a leadership pipeline; the nature to inspire followership; good judge of and magnet for talent

- Effective communicator across diverse constituencies—shareholders, clients, associates, financial community, etc.

- Candid, tough-minded, fact-based decision maker

- Self-aware and well-adjusted person

- Strategic thinker with proven intellectual skills

- Trusted; unquestionable integrity

STEP 3—SETTING UP THE PROCESS

Two tracks were established for the process, internal and external. At some point they would merge during the planned eighteen-month process.

The internal track would consist of the following steps:

- Competency-based interviews of the internal candidates against the CEO candidate profile

- An executive assessment based on the proprietary "Executive Intelligence" (ExI) diagnostic tool that complements competency-based interviews and references

- Board meeting to review and discuss the candidate assessments

- Individual board member sessions with the internal candidates

- Preparation of CEO visions by the internal candidates—what they would do as CEO of Major Global

- Board meeting at which each would present his or her CEO vision

- Additional due diligence as necessary

The external track would consist of developing a list of prospective candidates from outside the company that best matched the CEO profile. The prospects would be reviewed, along with detailed quantitative and qualitative performance analysis at a special board meeting. That was the point when the two tracks would merge. The internal candidates and external benchmarks would be compared, contrasted, and evaluated against the same selection criteria. If the board became convinced that the internal candidates stacked up favorably against the prospective outsiders, then they would continue the process of evaluating the insiders. If, however, the board either did not have confidence in the internal candidates or determined that there was demonstrably stronger and more appropriate experience on the outside, then the most qualified and interested external candidates would be approached and, if interested, brought in to meet with the board.

Detailed reference checks would be conducted, and final due diligence would then allow the board to make a determination as to who, on a risk-adjusted basis, would be the best leadership choice. With a candidate selected, the employment agreement would be negotiated, and a communications and transition plan would be developed; if all went smoothly, Major Global would have made the right choice using the right process.

STEP 4—INTERNAL TRACK

Internally there were three candidates with vastly different professional backgrounds that the board considered. One was Rachel Johnson, president of Major Markets and Global Services, Major Global's largest division. She was a brainy, Wesleyan University and Stanford Business School–educated, former Boston Consulting Group consultant who had been in the company since 2000. A second candidate was John Evans, president of National Account Services and International, the beloved operating whiz who had spent his entire career at the company since graduating from Rice University in 1983 and growing through progressively senior positions across all of Major Global's businesses. The third prospect was Charles McIntyre, a charismatic Californian, educated at Emory University and Harvard Business School, whose company was acquired by Major Global in 1996. Charles was the lone executive from that acquisition who remained at the company fifteen years later; after leading the postmerger integration, he rose to become head of the fastest-growing Small Business Services division.

The following is a snapshot of their professional backgrounds.

MAJOR GLOBAL, INTERNAL CANDIDATES

RACHEL JOHNSON	JOHN EVANS	CHARLES MCINTYRE
Location: New York, NY	Location: Alpharetta, GA	Location: Los Angeles, CA
Education: Stanford Business School, MBA, 1988 Wesleyan University, BA Economics, 1981	Education: Rice University, BS, 1983	Education: Harvard Business School, MBA, 1991 Emory University, BA, Government, 1986
Career History	**Career History**	**Career History**
2000–Pres: **Major Global Corporation** 2007–Pres: President, Major Markets and Global Services 2003–2007: President, Services	**1982–Pres:** **Major Global Corporation** 2008–Pres: President, National Account Services and International 2005–2008: President, National Account Services	**1996–Pres:** **Major Global Corporation** 2007–Pres: President, Small Business Services 2000–2007: President, Sourcing

Career History	Career History	Career History
2000–2003: Corporate Vice President, Strategic Development	2004–2005: President, Small Business Services	1997–2000: SVP and CFO, Simon Systems
1988–2000: Boston Consulting Group	2001–2004: Senior Vice President, Operations	1996–1997: VP, M&A, Simon Systems
1995–2000: Vice President	1999–2001: President, Consulting	1996–1996: VP, Operations, Simon Systems (acquired by Major Global)
1989–1995: Associate	1997–1999: Division Vice President, Southeast Division	**1994–1996: Simon Systems, Inc.**
1981–1986: General Electric Company	1995–1997: Division Vice President, Governmental Affairs	1994–1996: President
Corporate Audit Staff	1991–1995: Vice President, Information Services	1994–1994: CFO and COO
	1986–1991: Director, Client Services, National Accounts	**1991–1994: The Continent Group, Inc.**
	1982–1986: Manager, Administration and Services	CFO
		1990–1990: Goldman Sachs
		Summer Associate
		1986–1989: Chase Manhattan Bank
		National Banking Officer

Here is what the internal references, coaching feedback, and executive assessments indicated for each of the candidates' strengths and weaknesses.

RACHEL JOHNSON
Key Strengths

- Strong strategic, intellectual, quantitative skills honed at BCG

- Unquestioned values, ethics, and integrity; honest and trustworthy

- Expertise and passion for product-line strategy

- Strong M&A experience at Major Global; earlier at General Electric

- Understands the competitive environment, issues, and trends and the economics of the business

- Strong financial acumen

- Methodical, analytical, and fact-based decision maker

- Collaborative; team player

- Good communicator

- Deep experience with largest customer segment

Key Development Needs

- Limited operating experience, only six years of P&L responsibility

- Could be conflict averse

- Analytical skills often got in the way of decisiveness

- Sometimes slow to make the tough people decisions and hold people accountable

- Limited international operating experience; recently added responsibility for $300 million Canadian business

- Communications substance not always smoothly delivered

- Only fair executive presence; lacked "gravitas"

JOHN EVANS

Key Strengths

- Strong, results-driven operator, with deep domain knowledge of Major Global's businesses

- Broad and deep experience across all business segments; experience with turnarounds, growth, and postmerger scenarios

- Extensive track record of building successful teams in different businesses; tremendous followership and a significant network across the entire organization

- Respected for operating capability and results

- Bright and a quick study; energetic, committed, "can do," enthusiastic, positive, passionate and intense, results oriented

- Customer-centric; intense focus on new customer needs and service improvement

Key Development Needs

- Problem solving relied heavily on his instincts and deep knowledge of the business and the customers; limited strategic or analytical skills; sought patterns recognizable from past experience

- More a synthesizer of others' ideas than a thought leader himself

- Communications style was rapid-fire; he could be "all over the place"

- No exposure to balance sheet, treasury, or M&A

CHARLES MCINTYRE
Key Strengths

- Powerful strategic, financial, and operating skills

- Very quick study, incisive, with excellent critical-thinking skills; extremely intelligent

- Exceptional work ethic

- Strong business judgment and common sense

- Experienced managing through turnaround and growth, combining entrepreneurial and large corporate experience

- Outstanding operating skills and track record; hands-on and fair

- Excellent financial skills, including operating finance, treasury, IPO, and M&A

- Strong decision maker—blended facts, data, and analysis with instinct and common sense; decisive and directive

- Proven multicultural experience

- Outgoing personality, strong people skills, sharp sense of humor, good empathy; works well with others

- Strong executive presence and communicator

Key Development Needs

- Limited experience with Major and National Accounts divisions

- Tough, inquisitive style was abrasive to some, particularly within Major Global culture

- Could be impatient; chafed at the time needed to create major, organization-wide change

- Needed to continue forging bonds and building relationships with colleagues in other divisions

These strengths and weaknesses assessments, while very important when selecting a new leader, are only a first step. It is also valuable to make comparisons, by analyzing the relative strengths and weaknesses of the alternatives in the context of the needs of the organization. The board's in-depth discussion about Rachel, John, and Charles was framed by the following summary from the "Executive Intelligence" assessments:

INTERNAL CANDIDATE EXECUTIVE ASSESSMENTS

	RACHEL JOHNSON	JOHN EVANS	CHARLES MCINTYRE
Overall Assessment	**Exceeds executive norm** Highly analytic, intelligent, and intellectually honest leader; very strong practical intelligence, dissects complex issues, and identifies the core drivers of problems	**Exceeds executive norm** Above-average critical-thinking skills; accurately reads and responds to complex interpersonal and multiple stakeholder situations	**Greatly exceeds executive norm** Very sharp, analytic, inquisitive, and creative with strong executive intelligence across the board; creates effective processes to ensure efficiency and consistency, even in ambiguous/complex situations
General Business Analysis	**Greatly exceeds executive norm** Applies strong logic skills to guide decisions; strong ability to break down business tasks, identify critical objectives, and determine the best path to achieve goals	**Meets executive norm** Approaches complex problems by brainstorming, putting all options on the table, and selecting what he believes to be optimal; more a synthesizer of others' ideas than a thought leader	**Greatly exceeds executive norm** Strong ability to break down business problems, identify critical objectives, and determine best path to achieve goals

	Meets/exceeds executive norm	**Exceeds executive norm**	**Exceeds executive norm**
Interactive Awareness & Response	In highly complex interpersonal situations, with competing multiple agendas, frames issues accurately and discerns each stakeholder's approach; although she has a tendency to avoid confrontation	Socially and politically savvy, anticipating direct and indirect consequences of actions in complex interpersonal situations	Socially and politically savvy, quick to recognize the underlying motives and biases of others
	Exceeds executive norm	**Meets executive norm**	**Exceeds executive norm**
Self-Evaluation & Adjustment	Sharp analytic skills and common sense allow her to envision highly innovative solutions to difficult challenges; however, tends to spend slightly too much time defending views	Can be somewhat dismissive of alternative approaches; usually when he encounters superior arguments, he listens, comprehends, and eventually incorporates the strongest suggestions	Strong practical intelligence and open-mindedness create impressive ability to recognize and comprehend the complex ideas of others, even when they differ with his stated views

You can see that Charles greatly exceeded the executive norm with his sharp, analytic, inquisitive, and creative mind and his ability to create effective processes to ensure efficiency and consistency. From this analysis and the ensuing discussion, the board came to the point of view that while all three were strong internal candidates, Charles was in the lead. He had the best strengths and development needs assessment, and his executive intelligence results most consistently exceeded the norm for CEO and top-level executives against the key categories. The board, however, was urged to resist the natural temptation to jump to conclusions prematurely. Unlike the impromptu selection process of Roger five years earlier, the Major Global board had the time to let the process unfold.

STEP 5—EXTERNAL TRACK

The external track started with research to identify likely target companies in the sectors of relevance to Major Global. The research road map in the search for external candidates must be based on the experience and leadership requirements described in the candidate profile (step 2). Since the company was a leader in its industry and in healthy condition with three strong internal candidates, it was agreed that to even consider any prospective external candidates, they would need to have a proven track record of success as CEO or chief operating officer of a successful public company in the business services and technology sectors. As one director said, "The only reason to seriously consider going outside is if we can find a proven

CEO who has 'been there and done that' who would accelerate our transition by five years," relative to appointing a first-time CEO. "Why would we go outside for a first-time CEO," he continued, echoing what the rest of the directors were thinking when discussing the external track, "if we have three strong internal potential first-time CEOs?"

Six prospective outsider candidates were identified from the broad research exercise. This is a much shorter "long list" than a typical external track or full executive search. The reason was that the specificity of the criteria that composed the candidate profile and the up-front investment to diagnose the current and likely future states of the company enabled the board to be more targeted in considering prospects.

The yield of actual candidates from a typical long list who become interested in the opportunity and who after being interviewed and assessed are met by a board as fully vetted interested candidates is between 20 and 30 percent. The yield is primarily a function of four factors:

1. How fundamentally attractive the opportunity is—if you got a call to become the CEO of Google, you would probably be all ears.

2. How well matched the long list is to the opportunity—the list should be spot-on, and it should make sense why someone on the list could be interested. This is also related to how confident the search committee or hiring executive is that the list represents the very best and

most relevant prospects in the market. The less convinced they are, the longer the list needs to be.

3. Preexisting relationships with the prospective candidates—*who* makes the call really makes a difference. If you get a call from someone you know and trust to look at an opportunity, you will be much more likely to consider it than if you got a cold call from someone you never heard of or from an unknown company.

4. The stature and selling skills of the person presenting the opportunity to the prospective candidate—if the president of the United States asked you to become chief technology officer of the nation in order to bring America's competitiveness back to the best in the world, you would take the request very seriously, even if it meant taking a pay cut of 90 percent and relocating from your beloved Silicon Valley to Washington, DC. However, if someone you did not know from an organization you had barely heard of called you to test your interest in becoming the head of IT for the largest technology bureaucracy in the world, the US government, for $125,000 and it would require uprooting your family and moving across the continent, you would probably have a different reaction. While the comparison is exaggerated, it makes the point that *who* calls and *how* the caller presents the opportunity affect the yield dramatically.

FOR EACH OF THE six prospective external candidates, there was an in-depth discussion of their experience and accomplishments relative to the Major Global candidate profile. A quantitative and qualitative assessment was performed of their executive performance, including share price performance relative to competitors', revenue and profit growth, corporate reputation, track record of innovation, and external reputation in the market.

STEP 6—DECISION TIME

When the board met, it was time to take stock of where the succession process stood. It was clear that Charles McIntyre had emerged as the lead internal candidate. The question was how he compared to the best prospective candidates from outside the company. In a three-hour meeting, the board was led through a discussion of the six external prospects. Widespread consensus emerged around a candidate named Alistair Newcomb, CEO of "Sonic Systems and Services Inc." (SSS), as the external candidate of greatest interest to the committee. His experience lined up extremely well against the competencies called for in the CEO candidate profile:

- *General Management/CEO Track Record*: Under Alistair's leadership, SSS had been significantly transformed to regain a leading position in the software, services, hardware, and communications sector. His focus on improved client satisfaction and operational effectiveness and the acquisition of a key competitor led to impressive financial returns.

The stock price had grown notably, resulting in a greater than 50 percent increase since Alistair took over as CEO. Furthermore, he produced a remarkable growth in net income, increasing profits by 250 percent. Earlier, at "Allied Technology," as president, Alistair's key accomplishment was putting in place a program to accelerate growth in the company's largest business. Specifically, he built a strong, new leadership team and reorganized the sales force to effectively distribute a broad product line and grow market share, cutting the time to install new products in half. At both Allied Technology and SSS, Alistair had extensive experience serving premier global enterprises; SSS provides services to about ten thousand clients.

- *Technology*: At SSS, Alistair successfully led the company's development of market-leading research and development in cloud computing applications for the hardware and communications clients. At Allied Technology, Alistair had been responsible for running the IT function across the company.

- *Mergers and Acquisitions*: Alistair led SSS's major acquisition of its smaller rival, also based in San Jose, CA, in an all-cash deal worth $760 million, or $10 per share. Alistair had further experience in deals and deal structure through divestitures at SSS, including the sale of its small business portfolio.

- *Global Experience*: At SSS, Alistair oversaw the company's services in eighty countries. He traveled more than a hundred days per year and had been well received in both European and Asian cultures, according to references.

- *Leadership*: Alistair was a highly intelligent and strategic leader who developed into an effective hands-on operating CEO as well. He had a blend of entrepreneurial skills, blue-chip strategy training, and disciplined process management.

Beyond this experience, Alistair's performance was strong when measured by both the quantitative and qualitative factors:

- *Quantitative*: During Alistair's tenure, SSS Inc. achieved 54 percent share price growth, relative to a 1 percent drop in the broader market. Alistair also grew the company's total revenues by 38 percent and increased net income by 250 percent in just over five years.

- *Qualitative*

    - *Corporate reputation*—SSS was considered one of the world's leading information technology software and services firms. It was well known for its analysis tools and its authoritative IT knowledge. The company was routinely voted "most admired" and one of the "best places to work" by leading business publications.

    - *Innovation*—SSS had developed a new suite of products and services designed to serve the growing technology and information needs of clients around the world. They had won "best in show" at several leading technology conventions in the past twelve months.

- *Executive reputation*—-Alistair was highly regarded in the global technology industry as a thought leader. He had been described as having a "take no prisoners" management style that worked well in revitalizations and high-stakes M&A.

THERE WAS A great deal of confidence that Alistair would be interested in the Major Global CEO opportunity. He had been recruited to the board of directors of a large communications company, "Jupiter Networks," and in those discussions he confided that for the right opportunity he would consider leaving SSS. That opportunity would be to become CEO of a much larger company with a strong market position and a location that would be agreeable to his wife. Major Global was in fact three times the size of SSS, and its headquarters was located close to where Alistair's wife's family lived.

Alistair would have been a strong contender for sure. But the assessment came down to Major Global's position as a company both healthy and strong. Things got really focused when the chairman of the search committee asked the following question point-blank: "Based on all of our discussions and all of your experience, what is Spencer Stuart's recommendation?" On a risk-adjusted basis, Charles was the right choice to become Major Global's next CEO. The research pointed to the stronger performance of insider CEOs *when a company is healthy and growing* and of course when there is the availability of a viable internal candidate. This was very much the case with Major Global and Charles. The company was healthy as evidenced by the company situation assessment. Charles was a strong candidate based on his executive assessment, which showed that he exceeded or greatly exceeded the norms for top-level executives. Charles was known for his powerful strategic, financial, and operating skills, his incisive intelligence and excellent critical-thinking skills all turbo-charged by his huge work ethic. He was well accepted by the other leaders inside the company resulting from his successful track record, hands-on management style, and reputation as a nonpolitical, fair, and balanced manager. Finally, his multicultural experience, outgoing personality, and sharp sense of humor all combined to ensure that he would be a popular choice across the organization. Significantly, since he was already well accepted as a leader inside the company, there was virtually no cultural risk of promoting him to become CEO.

Alistair Newcomb, for all his relevant experience, proven success, and external visibility as a well-known CEO of a successful global software and services company, was a cultural risk. As a market leader with a strong internally focused culture, there was a nontrivial chance that Major Global would not embrace him as the new leader. "Why do we need to bring in an outsider," many would say, "when we're doing well and have Charles, John, and Rachel?" People would key in on Alistair's reputation as a "take no prisoners" manager, the kind of thing that would light up the Internet, on employee blogs, Twitter, and Facebook.

The Major Global chairman then announced that he was going to go around the board table and ask each director to express his or her point of view. One director after another articulated the case for Charles. As so often is the case in group dynamics, the momentum for Charles accelerated as each ensuing director articulated his or her views. Toward the end of the round-the-table discussion, directors were already starting to talk about the timing of the handover and the communications plan, rendering the unanimous decision complete. The chairman closed the meeting by asking Roger, the incumbent CEO, to share his thoughts.

"I've never been more proud," Roger said in a tone reminiscent of an NFL coach in the locker room after winning the Super Bowl. "This board has made a momentous choice, and it has chosen wisely. Our search committee is to be congratulated on leading an outstanding process that took nothing for granted and that did not presuppose any outcome. Our internal candidates were put through their paces, and each has grown over the course of these past months. Major Global is the better for it. We looked at the market and were able to see the very best external talent, and while there are some strong leaders whom we could have imagined coming in and doing a fine job, I think we all came to the same conclusion that the space between Charles and anyone from the outside was not sufficient to warrant taking that path. I am very happy . . . and my wife will be even happier!"

Congratulations were given all around and even a few backslaps as everyone got up from the table. The final step in the process was to communicate the decision to Charles, Rachel, and John, which was not altogether straightforward. The conversation with Charles, in particular, required careful scripting.

Here is how Roger presented the board's decision to Charles:

> I want to update you on the most recent conversations we have had with the board on the subject of CEO succession planning and our proposed next steps. The board is very pleased with your business results, with the way you have reacted to the feedback from me and from the 360 process, and with the results of the external executive assessment. You have emerged as the candidate of choice to succeed me as CEO. Congratulations!
>
> Everyone feels that you have the intellect, the drive, the business acumen, and the operating skills that the CEO position demands. In addition, the board and I feel that an internal successor is the ideal outcome from this process. In the time before I retire, I will get you more engaged with Wall Street and with our own board. We are going to expand your responsibilities to include all three divisions reporting directly to you. Between these new responsibilities and these exposures, your agenda will be demanding, but I am certain that you will be able to manage it.
>
> I'm sure that the past few months have been wearing on you, but the board is very pleased with how you have handled the pressure. This has been a rigorous process and one in which we believe all the steps were necessary. You

will have an opportunity to be Major Global's CEO for a long time so I encourage you to look at it as a long-distance race, not as a sprint. Well done, Charles!

As far as John and Rachel were concerned, John, the consummate operating executive, was given a broader business to run, which positioned him to become Charles's chief operating officer in time. Rachel, however, the superior strategist and multi-industry professional, was given the tough message that her future was not to be with Major Global. Importantly, this news was delivered with great care and a significant financial settlement—the accelerated vesting of her accumulated stock options and restricted stock, two years of base salary and bonus, and a smooth transition plan supported by a savvy public relations and corporate communications plan.

12. GOING WIDE: USING THE THREE ESSENTIAL TRUTHS IN EVERYDAY DECISION MAKING

The leadership selection approach using the three essential truths that we've detailed in this book can be applied in a stunningly wide variety of people decisions. The methodology of looking at a leadership need as one piece in a dynamic and interdependent puzzle, diagnosing what is required, and then finding the very best person through an inclusive and rigorous process works for choosing CEOs, members of an organization's senior leadership team, and a very broad array of other roles.

At an early 2011 meeting of the board of a Park Avenue New York City co-op apartment building, Harold Citrin (father of James and an early reader of this manuscript) used a lesson from *You Need a Leader—Now What?* in the board's search for a new building superintendent.

The real estate company that was the managing agent of the building offered the board eight candidates from which to choose, along with résumés for each. For the prior six months, however, one of the building's handymen had served as interim super. Some on the board were arguing that they should forgo the external candidates and simply give the interim super the permanent job, given that he was doing a good job in an acting capacity. Others were only interested in the external candidates with prior superintendent experience. Rather than force a decision at that meeting, which was how the agenda had been set, Citrin suggested that the board select the top three or four résumés and interview them along with the interim super, and select the candidate who best met the building's requirements. This recommendation struck the group as inarguably logical and fair and it was roundly accepted, which brought decorum back to the board.

Over the ensuing three months, the board was able to witness and interact with the interim superintendent with fresh perspective through the lens of his being a serious candidate for the permanent position. They also interviewed three external candidates, all with full building superintendent experience. Despite the similarity of the candidates' professional experiences, the board was struck by how different the cultural contexts were in which each worked. One candidate wanted to leave his building to escape a cantankerous relationship between the maintenance staff and the doormen, who were represented by a different union. Another was a super in a condominium, which had an entirely different environment from the tight-knit community feeling of the co-op. The third had good experience from a different Park Avenue co-op and seemed to have all the right personal attributes, but it was hard to know for sure how he would operate over time.

When it came time to decide, the board discussed how smooth the building had been operating in recent months, how the interim super seemed to have won the trust of his former peer maintenance workers, and how well he related to the building staff. They also considered the risks and disadvantages of bringing in someone from outside the building. These included losing the interim super, whose now nine months of proven experience would make him an attractive candidate for another building, and the questions of whether an outside candidate would relate well to the building's owners and other employees or upset the carefully developed culture of the building. So in the end, the decision was easy. With unanimity they chose the inside candidate and promoted the interim superintendent to the permanent position.

The board of trustees of one of the best liberal arts colleges in America illustrates yet another way in which the approach of this book can be applied in varied settings. To help its search for new trustees, the board made changes to its nominating process and other governance practices in order to follow the best practices of both for-profit and not-for-profit organizations. In line with the trend of more diligent corporate governance, the board also increased the transparency of and participation in the processes.

The trustee nominating process started with articulating the role of the board: to ensure and enhance the overall quality of the college for all its constituents—students, faculty, alumni, administration and staff, and the community at large. To dispatch these responsibilities, the board needed to be composed of a group of talented individuals of the utmost quality, integrity, diversity, and devotion to the college. The governance called for a board of up to thirty-five trustees, elected in two different ways: brought forth by the nominations committee to the full board, and nominated by the alumni association and elected by the alumni body independently of the board. Each trustee is elected to a term of four years and can be nominated to stand for reelection for a maximum of two additional consecutive terms. In practice, this means that trustees serve between four and twelve years. With these terms and term limits, steady turnover on the board is assured as well as the introduction of new experience and fresh perspectives. On average, three to four new trustees are elected annually.

The nominations committee established explicit selection criteria for new trustees as a guide to set priorities for the board and against which to evaluate potential candidates. These criteria are updated annually to keep the priorities fresh and to provide direction to the entire board. Potential trustee candidate ideas come from multiple sources: the full board, which is one important reason why the criteria are circulated; the president and development office, who regularly come into contact with alumni, parents, and friends of the college on campus and around the world through regional programs and alumni events; and the college relations office, which is in the constant flow of media and information concerning the college community. Identified names are researched, and those who seem promising are discussed at the nominations committee meetings, which take place as a part of each of the three board meetings held each year. Individuals' engagement with the college is considered, as well as the level and consistency of their financial contributions, their area of professional expertise, graduating year, and geographic, ethnic, gender, and racial diversity, among other factors. The top priority prospects are then reviewed in writing with the full board seeking comments, which are shared on a confidential basis back to the committee. If the feedback from all of this is positive, then the president, chairman of the board, or member of the nominations committee seeks to meet with the individual and proposes a trusteeship. When the prospect responds enthusiastically, the person's candidacy is moved to the full board for a vote, and when elected, the individual begins his or her four-year term.

Following were the college's key trustee selection criteria:

PROFESSIONAL CHARACTERISTICS

- Leadership and renown in a professional discipline of relevance to the college, consistent with the goals for balance among the following: Academia, Arts, CEO, CFO, Financial Services/Private Equity/Investments, Government, Technology, Legal, Media, Real Estate, Public Service

DEMOGRAPHIC CHARACTERISTICS

- Geographic Balance: Metro New York, Philadelphia, Washington, DC, Midwest, Southeast, Mountain States/ Pacific Northwest, California, International

- Balance across graduating classes from the 1940s to the 2000s

- Racial, ethnic, and gender diversity

PERSONAL CHARACTERISTICS

- *Engagement with the College.* A demonstrated history of involvement with and connection to the college; someone who has made a positive impact on the college in such areas as the annual alumni fund, alumni programs, career development, reunions, and so on.

- *Financial Means.* The potential to make leadership gifts and/or the commitment to give according to one's means.

- *Intellectual Prowess.* A penetrating thinker who can add value to the college's key strategic, operational, financial, and organizational issues and challenges.

- *Strong Verbal Communications Skills.* The ability to present ideas in a compelling, persuasive, and concise manner.

- *Exceptional Listening Skills.* The ability to absorb complex and interdependent information.

- *Collegial Personality.* The disposition to work effectively as a part of a group, whether in committees or the full board.

- *Curiosity.* The interest in continuous learning and the desire to take advantage of the college's academic offerings in periodic board settings.

- *Integrity and Ethics.* An unquestioned reputation for ethics, integrity, and honesty.

Prospective Trustee	Professional Discipline	Gender	Diversity	Geography	Engagement with the College	Intellectual Prowess	Financial Means	Other Personal
ROGER								
ROSIE								
BILL								
LUCY								

CANDIDATE EVALUATION

As a practical way to assess trade-offs among potential candidates, the nominations committee rates each prospect in a matrix fashion to prioritize and make final decisions.

Whether for a not-for-profit board, a major corporation, a family business, a school, or any other organization, when you have important people decisions to make, the leadership selection approach put forth in *You Need a Leader—Now What?* can be adapted and applied.

13. PITFALLS: AVOIDING THE TOP TRAPS IN LEADERSHIP SELECTION

Mistakes are avoided through experience; and experience comes from making mistakes. It is always preferable, however, to cut this process short by learning from the mistakes of others. If following the three essential truths detailed in this book is the best way to choose the right person for a top leadership position, then the inverse is also true. You can make costly errors by either failing to accurately diagnose the situation, by letting red herrings or other so-called rules get in the way of choosing the right person, or by failing to set and follow a rigorous disciplined process.

A key to conducting a successful leadership selection process is to recognize the most common problems and to be vigilant about steering clear. The following statements and subsequent commentary represent the six top pitfalls to be aware of and avoid.

1. "HIS CHARISMA WAS INTOXICATING"

Of course his charisma was intoxicating! That's what charisma is, and that's what charisma does. But having "a personal magic of leadership arousing special popular loyalty or enthusiasm"

(*Merriam-Webster*) or possessing the "trait found in individuals whose personalities are characterized by a powerful charm" (*Wikipedia*) does not make someone the right person for a position. We have seen leadership appointments go awry by being overly swayed by candidates with charismatic magnetism. While it is impossible and frankly wrong to ignore charisma in making people decisions, be aware of what it is and is not.

Recognize that charisma is like nectar on a flower attracting bees for pollination. It is attractive and draws you in, but all the same, it is a personal attribute, just like height, eye color, or left-handedness. Charisma can surely be a valuable trait in interpersonal situations as varied as general management, customer service, raising money from investors, public speaking, and of course sales. But it should not overwhelm having the right other qualities and experiences to fit into your organizational jigsaw.

One media company selected a charismatic head of advertising sales who was a prodigious revenue producer at another media company. She was commonly described as someone who "lights up a room when she walks in." A very compelling candidate. The problem was that whereas this trait was a key ingredient to her personal commercial success, it had nothing to do with critical parts of the job, which were more about strategic, operational, and people leadership. Her charisma did not help her develop a sales strategy for the organization, develop pricing policies, or select other people for key positions. She ended up being conflict averse and poor in giving performance reviews. In less than a year the best salespeople had left the company, and those who remained were not a happy lot. In the end, she turned out to be the wrong choice for that role, and the mistake could be traced directly back to making the hiring decision based on her compelling charisma.

2. "WE DON'T WANT ANY FAILURES"

Past performance is the best indicator of future success, right? It is hard to disagree with this notion, and it is in fact accurate to make performance assessments based on someone's tangible achievements and impact. However, this is not at all the same thing as eliminating candidates who have experienced a setback or, worse, an abject failure. Considering only people whose career trajectories have been a straight line of successes is dangerous business. Of course, no one wants to pick "a failure." But it may well be *your* situation where the candidate crashes and burns for the very first time. Not only that, it will at the very least limit your pool of potentially attractive candidates. The keys to avoiding this pitfall are to assess mistakes carefully and to focus as much on the competencies that will be required for success in the position you are deciding on.

For years an executive in the global technology industry had been considered one of the most sought-after candidates for top leadership roles. He had a steady rise through a major company's sales and field operations organization with experience on three continents. He was known for his inspirational leadership and devotion to solving his customers' toughest problems. He was happy at his company but open to hearing about the most attractive opportunities in other organizations. And the calls came in consistently, from venture capital firms, private equity investors, public company board directors, and executive recruiting firms—that is, until he had a falling-out with the company's founder and was forced to resign from the company. The incoming inquiries all but dried up. The investors and recruiters who had said, "Tell me when you're ready to make a change," didn't return his calls.

It is said that history is written by the victors. This is true in the world of executives as well. When someone is released from a position, it is usually assumed that the individual was at fault or, at best, that there are two sides to the story. But even if they know there is a chance that there is a sound explanation of what went awry, hiring managers are often reluctant to invest the time to figure out the other side of the story. Or even if they do, they are reticent to take a risk on someone with a visible failure because it opens them up to criticism later on if it doesn't work. Betting on a candidate with a failure takes courage.

One company did take that risk and hired a particular technology leader. Initially there was surprise and skepticism. "How could they hire someone who failed in his last job?" But the company did its homework in the form of deep references and due diligence. They spoke to people not only on the individual's reference list but to many others who were not on the list. The nature of their inquiry was to understand the conditions that led his actions and decisions to not work and to delve deeply into the nature and personality of the company's founder and culture as well. There was no disputing the facts—a long track record of success followed by serious challenges in the company wrought by the economic collapse and new competition and then a precipitous ousting. But they concluded that what he attempted to do in his prior company that got him sideways was precisely what was needed in their company. His mistakes were "good mistakes"; there were no integrity issues nor was there a strategic misreading of the situation. Rather, his actions—to make several key top management changes, to reduce costs by closing a money-losing but historically important division, and to actually make a symbolic increase in product development investment while reducing top management compensation—were deeply at odds with the founder's views and elements of the corporate culture. The new company could live with that—in fact, that was exactly what the doctor ordered.

This was in contrast to the "bad mistakes" of another visible candidate. This person had led a company that also got into trouble during the economic crisis. In that case, the aggressive decisions he made—to cut investments in R&D, to withhold bonuses to the sales force, and to withdraw from several investment markets—actually resulted in the company outperforming the competition in the short term and led to the company's sale to a larger rival. However, he was not the candidate of choice because the new company determined he was too driven by Wall Street.

There is another important benefit to opening up your consideration set to candidates who have achieved significant setbacks. They are highly motivated to succeed. They are eager to reclaim their reputations. So you may get a potentially deeper reservoir of underlying motivation and work ethic. This is fine as long as the candidate learned the right lessons from the failure and the hiring manager makes an accurate assessment of why something went off the tracks and projects the action's decisions into the new context.

In general, to assess a person's setbacks or weaknesses, in addition to careful referencing you need to get beyond the stock answers to interview questions. "My greatest weakness is that I'm too competitive," or "I left due to strategic differences with my boss." Rather, you want to see a candidate reflect thoughtfully. One successful candidate was asked to explain an unusually short tenure, thirteen months, at a well-known company. "I made the decision to join that organization for what turned out to be the wrong reasons," he explained without defensiveness. "I analyzed the competitive position of the company. I evaluated the balance sheet and cash flow. I carefully considered the role and how it aligned to my experiences and strengths. I studied the proxy for the compensation philosophy and specifics. But after only three months, it dawned on me that there was one important thing that I overlooked in my deep dive of due diligence—the people! I looked around and noticed that I didn't have anyone inside the company whom I could consider a friend. It was a terrible people fit for me. Once I realized this, I understood why I was so unhappy and ineffective."

3. "WE THOUGHT WE REALLY KNEW HIM"

Gerry was a close friend from law school of Lindsay, the CEO. Their careers followed parallel paths from the halls of academia into major corporate law firms on the East and West

Coasts of the United States where they were both among the youngest partners ever elected. Gerry joined a financial services firm as associate general counsel, and Lindsay soon thereafter joined a global banking company as the number two in business development. They spoke every week and always had dinner when in each other's cities. They had even vacationed together with their families. Lindsay had moved from business development into finance, becoming the bank's chief financial officer and three years later CEO; and Gerry had moved from the legal department into operations, rising to become his firm's chief operating officer. A year after Lindsay was appointed CEO, she decided that she needed a business partner to help manage the organization and run the sprawling enterprise. In consultation with her board of directors, she determined that hiring a COO would be the ideal way to complement her strengths and ensure operational discipline for the company. No one was surprised when she said she knew the perfect candidate! Gerry could not have been happier to move over to become Lindsay's COO.

All went smoothly . . . for about a month. Lindsay went ballistic when she was blindsided about a major profile of Gerry in the *Wall Street Journal* only the day before it ran. Lindsay's management team was renowned for its extraordinary work ethic and the flatness of its organization structure—she had thirteen direct reports. She hosted a three-hour weekly management meeting during which all fourteen executives including Lindsay went around the table and reported on their most important priorities. People were updated and Lindsay was skilled at using the forum to make decisions. Gerry felt like a fish out of water in these meetings. He maintained his promise to Lindsay to "listen and learn" and not take over the meetings, which were the core management process for the company. But he found the discussions terribly frustrating. They took a lot of time and were far too informal and conversational for his taste. At his prior company, as he stated a little too frequently, meetings were never more than ninety minutes, there was always a strict agenda, and the only people included were those considered central to making a particular decision. In fact, whereas Lindsay called her sessions "management meetings," Gerry had previously led what were called "decision meetings."

After a couple of months behind closed doors, he lobbied Lindsay to let him lead the meetings going forward. "How can you expect me to take the management burden off you and free you up for more important things like strategy," he reasoned, "if you don't let me do what you hired me to do?" So Lindsay announced that going forward Gerry would be leading the weekly sessions and that she would not attend so as not to "stifle the conversation." Despite his best efforts, it soon became evident that Gerry had little patience for the management meetings. He started circulating agendas a couple of days before each meeting and asked to preview presentations. He took what he considered these small and logical steps with genuine care to improve the meetings' efficiency and effectiveness. But still, the members of the management team were deeply resentful and described "a chill of hierarchy descending upon the company."

What came to undermine Gerry more than anything, however, was that people simply thought he didn't work hard enough. Lindsay and her leadership team were routinely in the office until 8 P.M. and in continuous contact by BlackBerry after hours and over weekends. Thanks to his organizational skills and devotion to work-life balance, Gerry, by contrast, was able to get his work done and left the office most days by 6 P.M. He checked his e-mail periodically, but he didn't want to encourage burnout-inducing 24/7 connectedness, so he was conscious not to be instantly responsive to the heavy weekend e-mail flow.

After a year, both Gerry and Lindsay reached the conclusion that it just wasn't working. They were both frustrated. Rather than achieving their goal of turning a close friendship into a successful business partnership, they had to decide whether their friendship could be salvaged. In postmortem interviews, it became clear to all concerned that what seemed like small stylistic differences actually reflected much deeper cultural and values differences. Lindsay's leadership team took great satisfaction in their inclusive, consensus-oriented management approach. Sure, decisions weren't necessarily reached as the straightest line between point A and B. But it worked for them. Their company was always considered excellent at execution, and it took Gerry's different approach for them to realize why. Whereas they may have been slower to reach big decisions, when they did, every area of the company was fully informed and bought in. So things really flowed. Gerry was widely respected and known to prize his family, fitness, and other interests outside of work. For him work was a means to an end. He could never really understand why people didn't want to do a great job in as short a time as possible so they could get on with "the important things in life."

It turns out that the frustrations on both sides, which at the surface seemed relatively trivial, actually reflected deep differences. It's therefore essential to probe deeply into the underlying values behind cultural norms to really make sure that even if you think you know someone, the cultural fit turns out to be right.

4. "WE NEVER REALLY AGREED ON WHAT WE WERE LOOKING FOR"

A not-for-profit institution was six months into a search for a new executive director to succeed a well-known and long-serving incumbent. They had seen an impressive, diverse, and unusually large slate of twelve candidates, but now the search was in disarray. Just a few days before the lead candidate was to have received an offer, he informed the hiring committee that he decided to withdraw from the process. The members of the team were devastated because he was a much stronger candidate than the backup and now they would have to restart the search from scratch.

In private conversation with the candidate, he said that he decided to not go forward because the more time he spent at the institution, with directors and with members of the leadership team, the more he concluded that there was fundamental disagreement as to what they were all looking for. He believed that without alignment about the direction and priorities for the institution, he would be both ineffective at and frustrated trying to lead the organization. He pointed out that some on the hiring committee were vocal about the fact that they were looking for a prominent visionary with global renown who could bring prestige, attention, and money to the institution. Their conviction was that this kind of candidate would create an exciting conception of where the world was going and catalyze the staff, board of directors, and the institution's donors to raise significant funds for the endowment. They wanted a "Mr. Outside" who would travel the world speaking at important conferences and be both comfortable with and effective at developing major donations and financial support.

There was an equally strong view from others on the committee and within the organization that "The last thing they needed was *another* visionary," referring to the prior director. They stressed that they needed someone to get the institution's operational house in order by hiring the right people, and then developing and mentoring them to ensure they were doing what was necessary to fulfill the organization's mission. They wanted someone who could return the institution to a balanced budget. In short, this group was looking for a "Mr. Inside" to make the trains run on time.

The candidate was not unique in being repelled from the director's position by a divided sense of what the organization and those responsible were looking for. Even potentially attractive leadership opportunities, such as top jobs at major media and retail companies, have gone vacant for up to twenty-four months because candidates perceived that there was disagreement among those responsible for the hiring.

What to do, then, to mitigate this risk? Before the hiring process begins, invest the time to discuss openly what you are looking for. Utilize the process of developing a position description to bring the group together around a common situation analysis and set of selection criteria as was done by Coastal Orthopaedics, the New York Public Library, PBS, and Major Global. What if you are part of a hiring team in the midst of a process already troubled due to disagreement over what you are looking for? First, recognize the importance of the issue. If the divide cannot be resolved, it will almost surely repel the most attractive candidates. Second, take a timeout in the process and gather everyone involved in the leadership selection to have a frank discussion about points of agreement and disagreement. Isolate and try to agree on the areas and attributes that are essential, the "must-haves," and be explicit about others that are important but "nice-to-haves." Third, if trying to achieve consensus around the criteria still doesn't work, then consider using a scenario analysis approach with the hiring team. For example, ask one another what the organization is likely to look like in five to seven years under the leadership of alternative candidate profiles. When considering different candidates whom the group has met, push yourselves to describe what would have to happen to make different particular candidates successful in the position over time. Done right, this will show where the gaps are and how likely it is that they can be closed.

5. "WE DIDN'T HAVE TIME TO RUN A THOROUGH PROCESS"

A driver's education video shows that for a typical suburban trip of five miles, the difference between one driver speeding, running through all yellow lights, and weaving in and out of traffic and another driving conservatively at the speed limit is about seven minutes. If you happen to be the speeder, your marginal time savings will quickly be eaten away if you are stopped and given a traffic citation.

So too is this the case with choosing the best person for an important leadership position. If you are so rushed that you feel it is necessary to eliminate a thorough process, keep the driving metaphor in mind. It may save you "minutes" by not involving enough of the right people up front, or by hiring the first candidate for the job without having considered alternatives, or by skipping the often time-consuming step of conducting detailed references. But these short-term time-savers are more than likely to cost you "hours" or "days" in the long run in terms of hiring mistakes or insufficient buy-in of a decision.

Consider the outcome in this example. The CEO of a large diversified technology company was frustrated with the perennially lackluster performance of one of his divisions. There was a strong engineering culture in the business and there had been significant turnover at the top of the organization. If it became known that the corporate CEO was going to replace the division chief, it would be the third time in three years that the division would have a new leader, destabilizing the management team and employee base and exacerbating the division's underperformance. So the CEO took it upon himself to find a world-class general manager to bring sound operational and cost management to the business. He met with a couple of candidates alone over a two-month time frame and decided whom to hire.

When it was announced that the division had another new boss, this time from outside of technology, the organization went nuts. People complained, the phones lit up, and e-mails flew around that corporate didn't get their business, that no one in the divisional management team could respect a non-engineer from an industrial company. Try as he might, the new division chief was not able to win over the management team. He simply did not have credibility, and the organization felt that he was thrust upon them. When long-serving senior members of the division got in touch with the functional leaders at the parent company, such as the global head of human resources, the corporate chief financial officer, and the general counsel, they learned that the appointment was a surprise to them, too. Having decided that speed and confidentiality were more important than buy-in, the CEO had kept his own counsel. With all the right intentions of hiring someone with the competencies he believed were most needed to turn the division around, he ended up making a crucial judgment error about the division's lack of receptivity to a nontechnology leader. Not only was he not the right person for the job, but the lack of any process doomed the new manager from the start.

It would have been ideal to have members of the divisional management team meet the prospective leader from a buy-in point of view. But that usually doesn't work either for confidentiality reasons or because it creates an unhealthy dynamic where managers have the potential to veto the hiring of their next boss. In this case, the problem could likely have been avoided by including more people (e.g., functional leaders at the parent company) on the interview panel.

When you are selecting a person for a new leadership position, even if it's an internal candidate, think carefully about all the people whom the individual will have to work with in order to thrive. Then involve them in the formation of the position specification and key selection criteria and have them meet candidates along the way. This will dramatically improve the success rate at choosing just the right individuals for your most important and influential leadership positions.

6. "LET'S BRING IN A NUMBER TWO AND, WHEN HE'S READY, PROMOTE HIM TO THE TOP JOB"

If you have to go outside your organization for a new leader, many believe that the person should be brought in through a two-step process: first as COO (or similar top role) and then promoting him or her to CEO within one to two years. On the surface it appears to be a logical way for an outsider to learn the business, become inculcated into the culture, and build key relationships. The surprising fact, however, is that this approach sets the new leader up for failure and rarely works.

A seventy-two-year-old company patriarch who had spent the better part of his life building his multibillion-dollar eponymous company made this pronouncement in a meeting with his human resources chief and external consultants: "I've decided it's time to bring in a new leader for the company. I don't want to run the day-to-day business anymore. But"—it was clear what was about to come on the other side of his pregnant pause—"I'm not sure I'm prepared to turn over the company from day one. Therefore, what I'd like to do is conduct a search for a chief operating officer, someone who will come in and work with me for a year or two as an apprentice, and if all goes well, promote him or her to CEO at that time."

Leaning into the conference room table, the chief human resources officer was aching to say what was on her mind. In the premeeting with the consultants, she had sounded the warning. The founder was grappling with the emotions of letting go and fixating on the questions of how to turn over the leadership mantle, to whom, and when. Now that the time had finally arrived to launch the succession process, he was equivocating. The mission was how to help get him back on track. "Sir," the adviser started respectfully, "we understand your dilemma. On one hand, you are ready for a new leader to assume the helm of this great company that you have worked so hard to build. But on the other hand, given the uniqueness of your business and the distinctiveness of your corporate culture, you are apprehensive about appointing a new CEO and giving over total control right from the start. This is a common way that people think about bringing in a new leader from the outside. There's just one problem. It usually doesn't work."

Known as "insider-outsiders," these "CEOs in waiting" reflect their circumstances of being within the company for a period of time, giving them insider status, but still being new enough to remain somewhat of an outsider as well.

As companies and boards work hard to be more strategic and proactive in their leadership selection and succession planning, we've seen an increase in the kinds of discussions as was had with the iconic company founder. We often have to discuss with our clients whether bringing in a COO with the intent of becoming a CEO successor is in fact a good strategy at all and, if not, why it doesn't work.

This two-step strategy suffers from five serious disadvantages:

- The candidates you will attract will not be as strong as those you would attract by bringing in a CEO out of the gate. It is difficult to find the right person who has the capability and experience to assume the top spot but who is willing to come in as a number two.

- The skills for success are different between a number one and number two. The CEO needs to be more strategic and externally facing, and the COO tends to be more internally facing while operational. It is rare to find the executive who is accomplished in both.

- When you bring in a COO or number two, the new executive does not benefit from having the change mandate typically granted to an outsider in the top job. It is difficult for a number two to make swift and unpopular people decisions and challenge long-held strategies and assumptions (that may have been associated with the incumbent CEO).

- Not only does he or she not have the benefits of being a true outsider, the new executive does not have the advantages of being an insider, either. The insider-outsider cannot rely on personal company knowledge or understand how decisions are made in the organization. Without the key internal relationships of an insider, it is much more difficult to lead effectively.

- Perhaps most debilitating, because a COO or president brought in as part of a two-step strategy is essentially in audition mode for the CEO post, the new executive is more likely to play things safe. It is only natural to try to avoid making mistakes that will prevent you from getting the top job. In the process, during this interim period, the new executive also has to be deferential to the CEO all while not being seen as milquetoast. The CEO still calls the shots and is the primary conduit to the board of directors, who will be evaluating the number two and determining when *and if* he or she will be ready for the job. Consequently, the new executive will go to great lengths to avoid getting on the wrong side of the CEO. And even after the two-step transition is complete, there are potential limits to the degrees of freedom the new CEO feels in how to lead the company. Because the insider-outsider was assimilated under the auspices of the incumbent, he or she may feel obligated to remain loyal to the vision, especially if the predecessor remains on the company's board after leaving the CEO office.

Michael Roth, the chairman and CEO of Interpublic Group (see pages 80–83) who successfully came off the company's board of directors to become chief executive, agrees that there are distinct challenges of such two-step appointees, especially "legacy issues" that have to do with separating themselves from the CEOs under whom they apprenticed. Roth believes that two-step transitions disable the new chief executive from making swift, necessary changes upon his or her appointment to the top job. "Because they were brought in and assimilated within the specific strategic direction of their predecessor," he explains, "they often feel obligated to remain loyal to this direction, more so than a pure outsider, or even an insider, by the way, who was never mentored as heir-apparent."

Even with all of this baggage and lack of evidence that these transitions are successful, two-step appointments continue to have their appeal to companies. They hope to minimize the "organ-rejection" risk of hiring an outsider and don't believe they yet have the appropriate internal talent. But hirer beware—a transition period is risky for the incoming executive and unstable for the organization. For a period of time, the majority of the risk is on the candidate's shoulders. Still, if you're committed to this approach, what to do?

You need to start by considering two ways to mitigate the risk to the candidate, both of which transfer the risk over to the company. The first is financial. Structure the employment contract such that if the executive is not promoted to the number one position within an agreed-on time frame, he or she will be eligible for a significant payment, not unlike a breakup fee in a merger agreement. The second way, which as of now is less common but potentially more effective, is through the commitment of a public announcement. At the time of appointment, announce the intention that the new executive will become CEO within a defined time period. The company may even use the title "CEO designate." The downside of this particular candidate risk-reducing action is that it accelerates making the CEO a lame duck. This is inevitable and making a publicly committed CEO designate may make it happen sooner than desired. However, this is a trade-off that may be worth making.

This is how Estée Lauder recruited Fabrizio Freda, one of the most highly regarded Procter & Gamble executives, into the company in March 2008. In the public announcement of the appointment, the company said that Freda would become president and chief operating officer and would succeed William Lauder, grandson of the company's founder, as chief executive officer within twenty-four months. What was so unusual about this public pronouncement was the long time frame that was set out for all to see. By all measures and according to a number of Estée Lauder board directors, the CEO transition, which was completed on July 1, 2009, well before the two-year "deadline," has worked brilliantly. Because of the inherent qualities and personality of Freda, the unambiguous signal to the organization of who was going to be in charge, and the grace by which chairman and now former CEO William Lauder trained and then deferred to Freda, the company responded smoothly to the change.

A third possible approach is to extend the time period between a potential CEO candidate's appointment to a number two role and his or her actual ascension to the helm of the company. Using a three- or four-year time frame, instead of a one-year to eighteen-month plan, for example, essentially makes the CEO candidate an insider and gives him or her sufficient time to establish an "insider" presence within the company. To make this work, it is essential to set the right expectations with the candidate—that is, striking the right balance of putting forth the possibility of succession in the medium term but *not* making it an explicit objective that risks setting up an audition mode.

CONCLUSION

Extending the Three Essential Truths Across
the Organization

One of the conclusions that we hope you will draw from *You Need a Leader—Now What?* is that both business and not-for-profit organizations are more multifaceted than ever, with complex interdependencies that are best thought of as a jigsaw puzzle. When leaders are in sync with the organization and the choice is right, positive energy is released and groups of people work collaboratively toward a common goal. But when wrong choices are made for key leadership roles, even if the individuals are perfectly good and talented, it is difficult for them and the organization to perform effectively.

This lesson is obviously not limited to the CEO and should be understood and applied throughout the organization. While the choice of top leaders has a disproportionate impact on the future success of the company or institution, there are many other important choices that are made at different leadership levels. For an organization to perform at its best, with productive employees who are motivated about their work, it is essential to make the right choice in each leadership decision. Applying the three essential truths of leadership selection throughout the organization will become a key competitive advantage.

With that idea in mind, there are several insights that we hope you will keep in mind when choosing a leader:

1. Remember to look at the person you are seeking to appoint only after considering the puzzle you are trying to solve. Consider the strengths and weaknesses of the team, where you want the organization to go, what skills will be required to get there, and what interpersonal characteristics are required to operate effectively within the cultural norms. While CEO succession will impact the entire organization, other people decisions create significant impact on the team, division, or group as well.

2. Having mapped out the puzzle, now identify the right piece by detailing the specific selection criteria and assessing each candidate against them. It is here that you want to be vigilant about challenging red herrings often dressed up as conventional wisdom, whether that be age, experience, or ethnicity.

3. Once the puzzle and pieces are identified for the right choice, then it is essential to deploy the right process. Of course, the approach of selecting a CEO is necessarily different from other positions across the organization, because it is the board rather than a hiring manager who leads the process. Just the same, the key principles about the right process apply equally, such as the importance of soliciting the input of key constituencies that will affect the success of the new employee, the need to structure candidate interviews properly, and the requirement

to be thoughtful about internal competition and visible horse races.

Everyone who is deciding whom to hire, or which organization to work for, is making his or her own choice. While all of the considerations that we put forth in this book are based on our research and experience with significant hires around the world, the most important choice for you personally may well be your own. Keep the three essential truths of leadership selection steadfastly in mind and let the *You Need a Leader—Now What?* approach help you choose wisely.

SOURCES

CHAPTER 1: THE CURIOUS CASE OF BILL PEREZ

"Nike's Chief to Exit After 13 Months—Shakeup Follows Clashes with Co-Founder Knight; Veteran Parker to Take Over," Joann S. Lublin and Stephanie Kang, January 23, 2006, *The Wall Street Journal*.

"Founder of Nike to Hand Off Job to a New Chief," November 19, 2004, *The New York Times*.

"Phil Knight Resigns Top Job at Nike," Anne M. Peterson, November 18, 2004, The Associated Press.

"Nike: Can Perez Fill Knight's Shoes? The 'Radically Different' Pick to Be the Outfit's New Chief Has to Adjust to an Insular Culture Where His Predecessor Is Lionized," Stanley Holmes, November 22, 2004, *BusinessWeek Online*.

"Inside the Coup at Nike," February 6, 2006, *BusinessWeek Magazine*, Commentary.

"Wrigley Names First Outsider to Run Company," October 24, 2006, *The Wall Street Journal* Asia.

"Wrigley's Bills: A Delicate Balance; Sharing Power Could Cramp First Outside CEO," Julie Jargon, October 30, 2006, *Crain's Chicago Business*.

"Wm Wrigley Jr Co Realigns Management in Commercial Operations," February 27, 2007, M2 EquityBites.

"A 'Home Run' for Wrigley: Foreign Sales Fuel Record 1st-Quarter Results; Shares Soar," John Schmeltzer, May 1, 2007, *Chicago Tribune*.

"Wrigley's Stick Gums to Receive Packaging and Flavor Makeover," March 13, 2008, Datamonitor News and Comment.

"For $23 Billion, Mars Now Owns Wrigley; Deal Creates World's Largest Candy Company," Cheryl V. Jackson, September 26, 2008, *Chicago Sun-Times*.

Interviews with Bill Perez.

Fact-checking conversation with Nigel Powell, SVP, Corporate Communications, Nike Inc.

CHAPTER 2: THE THREE ESSENTIAL TRUTHS FOR CHOOSING THE BEST PERSON FOR YOUR ORGANIZATION

Interviews with Dr. Jerome Barton, Coastal Orthopaedics.

"Time Inc. Chief Executive Jack Griffin Out," Jeremy W. Peters, February 17, 2011, *The New York Times.*

CHAPTER 3: *PATIENCE* AND *FORTITUDE*: THE NEW YORK PUBLIC LIBRARY PRESIDENTIAL SEARCH

NYPL press release; http://www.nypl.org/press/press-release/2010/10/06/new-york-public-library-names-dr-anthony-marx-next-president.

"Tiger of the Week: Anthony Marx *86 *90," Brett Tomlinson, October 13, 2010, *Princeton Alumni Weekly*, http://blogs.princeton.edu/paw/2010/10/tiger_of_the_we_50.html.

Interviews with Tony Marx, Joshua Steiner, Catie Marron, and New York Public Library staff.

Spencer Stuart case histories and research.

CHAPTER 4: THE APPOINTMENT OF A FIRST-TIMER

Interviews with Frits van Paasschen and Steve Quazzo.

Spencer Stuart case histories and research.

CHAPTER 5: USING EVIDENCE: LESSONS FROM THE CEO TRANSITION STUDY

"Nardelli Out at Home Depot; No. 1 Home Improvement Retailer Gives Ex-CEO $210 Million Package; Vice Chairman Frank Blake Takes the Helm," Parija B. Kavilanz, January 3, 2007, CNNMoney.com.

"Ending the CEO Succession Crisis," Ram Charan, February 2005, *Harvard Business Review.*

"CEO Succession 2008: Stability in the Storm," Summer 2009, Per-Ola Karlsson and Gary L. Neilson, *Strategy & Business.*

"The Turnover of Top Bosses Has Risen Alarmingly: A Survey of Corporate Leadership," October 23, 2003, *The Economist.*

"Succeeding at Succession," James M. Citrin and Dayton Ogden, November 2010, *Harvard Business Review*.

"Ford to Relinquish Control of Mazda Through Stake Sale," October 18, 2008, *The New York Times*.

ATP press release, "ATP Appoints Adam Helfant as New Executive Chairman & President," January 12, 2009.

"Helfant's Progress One Year into the Job," Tom Tebbutt, January 21, 2010, ESPN.com.

"Six Former Senior Executives of Xerox Settle SEC Enforcement Action Charging Them with Fraud," U.S. Securities and Exchange Commission, Washington, DC, Litigation Release No. 18174, June 5, 2003.

"The Accidental CEO: She Was Never Groomed to Be the Boss. But Anne Mulcahy Is Bringing Xerox Back from the Dead," Betsy Morris, June 23, 2003, *Fortune*.

"The 100 Most Powerful Women," August 19, 2009, *Forbes*.

Interviews with Anne Mulcahy and John Pepper.

"For Ford, the Road Ahead Is Full of Smaller Cars," Bill Vlasic, July 24, 2008, *The New York Times*.

"Advertising: Interpublic's Chairman Steps Up to Active Role in Rebuilding Firm," November 4, 2004, *The Wall Street Journal*.

"David Bell Not Asked to Return to Interpublic Board," October 21, 2005, *Chicago Business*.

"Michael Roth Named CEO at Interpublic; David Bell Will Serve as Co-Chairman," January 19, 2005, *Business Wire*.

"Networker: David Bell—Judgment Day," October 29, 2004, *Campaign*.

"The Turnaround Being Pursued at the Interpublic Group Remains a Work in Progress," April 6, 2005, *The New York Times*.

"Advertising: Interpublic's Chairman Steps Up to Active Role in Rebuilding Firm," November 4, 2004, *The Wall Street Journal*.

"Business Week Executive Profile: Michael Roth," http://investing .businessweek.com/businessweek/research/stocks/people.

"Media Operations Chief Named at Interpublic," May 13, 2005, *The New York Times*.

Interviews with Michael Roth.

CHAPTER 6: AVOIDING THE "RED HERRINGS" OF AGE, EXPERIENCE, AND ETHNICITY

"General Motors Hires Chris Liddell, CFO of Microsoft, as Its New Finance Chief," December 21, 2009, *New York Daily News*.

"Rugby Star Gets GM Out of a Scrum," Dennis K. Berman and Sharon Terlep, December 2, 2010, *WSJ Online*.

Interviews with Chris Liddell, November 2009, December 2010, January 2011.

"GM Finance Chief Liddell Resigns," Sharon Terlep, March 11, 2011, *WSJ Online*.

"Dr. Jim Yong Kim Appointed 17th President of Dartmouth College," March 2, 2009, Dartmouth College Office of Public Affairs.

"Kim Rekindles Dartmouth Alumni Amid Austerity Protest," Oliver Staley, September 8, 2010, *Bloomberg BusinessWeek*.

"Ivy League Applications Increase," Lindsay Brewer, January 28, 2011, *The Dartmouth*.

"Hispanic Trending. No Average Joe: Univision CEO Uva Gets Rave Reviews from Ad Community," May 26, 2008, *Broadcasting & Cable*.

"Q&A with Univision's Joe Uva. The Univision CEO Discusses How His Networks Are Mobilizing Hispanic Viewers to Pay TV and Courting $1 Trillion in Consumer Purchasing Power," April 5, 2010, http://qnnnews.wordpress.com/2010/04/05/qa-with-univisions-joe-uva/.

"Univision Seizes Viewer Milestone," September 9, 2010, *The Wall Street Journal*.

"Media Impact in NY and DC: Public Broadcasting Service," Paula Kerger, January 24, 2009, http://jmc346.blogspot.com/2009/01/public-broadcasting-service-paula.html.

CHAPTER 7: A LEADERSHIP SELECTION *TALE OF TWO CITIES*

Extensive interviews with board members and executives of the masked American industrial company.

Spencer Stuart case histories and research.

CHAPTER 8: THE POWER OF CONSTITUENCY INTERVIEWS

Interviews with Kevin Sharer.

Interviews with Paula Kerger and PBS staff.

Spencer Stuart case histories and research.

CHAPTER 9: WHEN TO USE A HORSE RACE

"Is a Horse Race the Best Way to Select a CEO?," James M. Citrin, July 27, 2009, *WSJ Online*.

"The Horse Race: High-Stakes Succession Planning," John Mitchell, July 2007, *Point of View*.

"Susan Arnold Exits a Top P&G Post, Narrowing the Race for Succession," Ellen Byron and Joann S. Lublin, March 9, 2010, *The Wall Street Journal*.

"Arnold Likely to Be Wooed for CEO Jobs," Ellen Bryon and Joann S. Lublin, March 10, 2009, *WSJ Online*.

"Robert McDonald: Executive Profile & Biography," January 16, 2011, *Bloomberg BusinessWeek*.

CHAPTER 10: ORCHESTRATING CANDIDATE INTERVIEWS

Interviews with Spencer Stuart consultants on best practices.

Spencer Stuart case histories and research.

CHAPTER 11: THE CASE OF MAJOR GLOBAL

Extensive interviews with board members and executives of the masked company, Major Global Incorporated.

Spencer Stuart case histories and research.

CHAPTER 12: GOING WIDE: USING THE THREE ESSENTIAL TRUTHS
IN EVERYDAY DECISION MAKING

Interviews with Harold Citrin.

Interviews with president, chairman, and nominating committee of the non-identified liberal arts college.

CHAPTER 13: PITFALLS: AVOIDING THE TOP TRAPS
IN LEADERSHIP SELECTION

Spencer Stuart case histories and research.

Spencer Stuart CEO Transition Study.

Interviews with Michael Roth.

ACKNOWLEDGMENTS

"And the Oscar goes to . . ."

This is about as close as we'll ever come to being able to take out the crinkly scrap of paper and publicly thanking the incredible people who have helped make this book a reality.

First, we would like to thank our friend and partner Ignacio Marseillan, who was with us in the summer of 2008 discussing the "insider-outsider" topic and suggested that we pursue the research and write the book. We would also like to thank our CEO, David Daniel, a Spencer Stuart "insider" if there ever was one, and our chairman, Kevin Connelly. Both are dear friends with whom we have spent nearly two decades working (and sometimes playing) together. They have been highly supportive of this project from day one and throughout.

If there were a third author on the cover of this book, it would surely be the inimitable Amanda Facelle. Possessing a brilliant research mind as well as a voracious work ethic and infectiously positive disposition, Amanda is a gifted writer whose contributions can be found on every page of this book. Recruited into our firm fresh off the campus of Wesleyan University in Middletown, Connecticut, she helped formulate and conduct the research that became the Spencer Stuart CEO Transition Study. She spent hundreds of hours on primary and secondary research, delving into each CEO transition in the United States and internationally. Amanda spent weeks at a time in different European capitals working with our partners there and conducting research and analysis. Partnering with Amanda over a two-year period were her fellow Spencer Stuart analysts, Kate Scrimale and Amanda Granson, to whom we are also deeply appreciative; they too performed extensive research on CEO transitions, and their work was central to the study and this book (Kate was recruited to Spencer Stuart straight from the University of Richmond and worked shoulder to shoulder with Amanda for the first year of the CEO Transition Study research before moving into our Consumer Goods Practice).

We would also like to thank our partners, mentors, and friends Tom Neff and Dayton Ogden. Tom and Dayton have been the role-model leaders for both of us and for our firm globally for over three decades. They are simply the most experienced experts on CEO succession, leadership selection, and the dynamics of recruiting top leaders of anyone in the world.

Our London-based partner and friend, Edward Speed, took the lead on designing and overseeing the European CEO Transition Study, and we are grateful for his devotion and leadership. At the country level, we would like to thank our partners Jonathan Smith in the United Kingdom, Bertrand Richard in France, Yvonne Beiertz in Germany, and Han van Halder in the Netherlands for their work. We also are grateful to Mark Stroyan and Simon Fenton, whose sponsorship of our European study was critical to its realization. Additional research and analysis behind the European CEO Transition Study was performed with excellence by Max Shaw in London (as an intern before his junior year at Princeton University) and Sue Ann Kim in Amsterdam.

Our friend and partner Greg Sedlock, a digital media expert in Stamford and student of leadership, was a critical thought leader in conceiving of, structuring, and executing the CEO Transition Study. He was also a consistent sounding board for the book and read and commented on many versions of the manuscript over the course of its development. Similarly, Ryan Eick, an enormously talented associate in Stamford who has embarked for his MBA at the University of Virginia's Darden School, was a central leader in the two-year CEO Transition Study. He developed the core research methodology, programmed the database, project managed the work effort, and helped train Amanda, Kate, and Amanda in how to analyze CEO performance. We would also like to thank Jim Billington, a senior finance executive at the firm, who is also a statistical guru, for helping the entire project team make sense of and draw the right conclusions from the mountains of data in our study.

Another core member of this effort to whom we owe a gargantuan debt of gratitude is our partner and friend Ben Machtiger, who serves as Spencer Stuart's chief marketing officer. Ben provided advice, guidance, support, and feedback (occasionally tough love) through the countless iterations of the manuscript development. He is a thought leader in his own right and a guiding light at Spencer Stuart.

Our partners in our various industry and functional practice groups devoted many hours to this book as well. They conducted and shared specialized research on leadership transitions in the education and sports sectors and among financial officers. They also reviewed relevant passages of the manuscript to make sure that our facts and conclusions were on target (although we assume full responsibility for any errors). Specifically, we would like to thank Jennifer Bol, Michele Haertel, and Mary Gorman, from our Education and Government Practice, Tom Daniels and Adam Kovach, from our Financial Officers Practice, and Jed Hughes and Phil Murphy, from our Sports Business Practice.

One final expression of Spencer Stuart gratitude goes to Karen Steinegger, who for over seventeen years has worked with Jim Citrin on all aspects of his work, including this book. She read various passages and provided her sharp insights as well as managed all the logistics behind the development of this book, from setting up interviews with CEOs, board members, chief human resources officers, to working sessions with the internal team and our partners at Crown Business. Thank you, Karen.

Outside of Spencer Stuart there are also a lot of people to thank. Scott Osman, Global Director, Corporate Social Responsibility at Landor Associates, is one of the sharpest thinkers in the world about business and marketing issues. Scott has been a major contributor to how our thinking has evolved over the course of this project. His conviction that we were onto some important and new insights about leadership selection and management with this book was critical encouragement to us when our spirits occasionally flagged. In addition, we want to express our thanks to Professor Jeffrey Sonnenfeld,

Senior Associate Dean, Executive Programs and Adjunct Professor, Management at Yale University Graduate School of Arts & Sciences, for inviting us into his leadership seminar for MBA students to share some of our early research with his talented and enthusiastic students.

Youngme Moon, author of what we believe is one of the best ever books on marketing, *Different—Escaping the Competitive Herd*, read an early version of our manuscript and provided some seminal advice. She implored us to be more declarative about what to do to make the right people decisions, buttressed by research, and to identify the "essential truths" about leadership selection. Her guidance shaped the direction of the book, and for that we are deeply appreciative.

Selecting the title of a book is one of the most difficult and—according to the book marketing experts—most important parts of publishing a book. Fairly late in our process, our friends Bob and Francine Shanfield suggested that we needed "something with a call to action." They asked, "Can't you do something like *You're in Charge, Now What?*" (referring to the 2003 book by Tom Neff and Jim). "We loved that title!"

Two days later, our client and friend Donn Davis, cofounder and president of Revolution LLC, was reviewing the manuscript and said that the most important part of our previous book title was not "You're in Charge" but rather "Now What?" With that insight we turned back to our extended book working team and it was Ryan Eick who finally came up with the lead-in that we ultimately selected—"You Need a Leader"!

We are also deeply appreciative to the executives who devoted their time discussing the concepts that formed this book and for sharing and reviewing their specific stories: Bill Perez; Josh Steiner; Catie Marron; Tony Marx; Deanna Lee, VP Communications, NYPL; Kevin Sharer; Katherine Lauderdale, Sr. VP, General Counsel & Corporate Secretary, PBS; Mary Bitterman; Paula Kerger; Michael Roth; Joe Uva; Jason Kilar; John Pepper; Jim Kim; Lou D'Ambrosio; Benito Cachinero; Frits van Paasschen; KC Kavanagh, SVP Global Communications, Starwood Hotels & Resorts; Steve Quazzo, Chairman of Starwood CEO Search Committee; and Dr. Jerry Barton.

Rafe Sagalyn is, in our humble opinion, the best literary agent on the planet. His patience and fortitude rival that of the NYPL lions. This is our sixth book together, and none would have ever happened without him. Thank you, Rafe.

If Rafe is the best literary agent, then John Mahaney is surely the best editor in the business. This book was a labor of love thanks to John; and like mothers bearing children, the labor could be painful. John challenged us for over two years to strike the right balance between specific insights about CEO succession and the much broader topic of how to choose the best people for important roles, regardless of where they sit in the organization or frankly what kind of organization it is. He restructured and restructured the manuscript, and when we thought we had it nailed, he restructured it some more. Our hope is that the final product will be so logical that as a reader you will wonder how it could have possibly been done differently. Also, the talented Crown Publishing team, led by Tina Constable, is always the ideal partner for a project like this; and we would like to thank Tara Gilbride, the inspiring and creative publicity director, and Meredith McGinnis, the

associate director of marketing, for their support, encouragement, and commitment.

Finally, we would each like to thank our families for their
love and support. The early hours of most weekend days and
vacations kept us away from our spouses, Gail Citrin and Bob
Daum, and from our beloved children, Teddy, Oliver, and Lily
Citrin and Alexandra, Schuyler, and Bailey Daum.

And just like the winner of the Oscar for excellence in
some obscure technical field goes painfully over his allotted
thank-you time, we too will now rush off to the after party!

INDEX